BRINGING
TUSCANY HOME

FRANCES MAYES

BRINGING TUSCANY HOME

SENSUOUS STYLE FROM THE HEART OF ITALY

WITH EDWARD MAYES

PHOTOGRAPHY BY STEVEN ROTHFELD

BROADWAY BOOKS   NEW YORK

BROADWAY

Printed in Japan.

BROADWAY BOOKS and its logo, a letter B bisected on the diagonal, are trademarks of Random House, Inc.

Visit our website at www.broadwaybooks.com

First edition published in 2004

Page ii: Fresco detail, Villa Corsini, Castello

Page v: Fresco detail by Jim Fodor at the home of Rupert Palmer and Donatella de Palme. Jim Fodor can be reached at 805-637-6305

Book Design by Nancy Campana/Campana Design

Food Styling (California) by David Shalleck

All photographs © 2004 by Steven Rothfeld except those on pages 84, 115 (lower photograph), and 224, which were taken by Frances Mayes.

Library of Congress Cataloging-in-Publication Data
Mayes, Frances.
    Bringing Tuscany home : sensuous style from the heart of Italy / Frances Mayes ;
  with Edward Mayes ; photographs by Steven Rothfeld.
      p.   cm.
    1. House furnishings—Italy. 2. Housekeeping—Italy. 3. Interior decoration. I. Title.

TX311.M393 2004
747'.0945—dc22   2004045690

ISBN 0-7679-1746-4

10 9 8 7 6 5 4 3 2 1

FOR
FULVIO DI ROSA

ACKNOWLEDGMENTS

Our thanks to Ashley, who brought Willie over to Italy three times in his first year and allowed us to feed him *ragù,* olives, and focaccia. Willie, our grandson, born in 2002, deepens our family commitment to living in two cultures. We are grateful for the chance to give him an Italian self. Ed, especially, thanks Todd Alden for great wine talk and many popped corks. Melva and Jim Pante, friends in San Francisco and Cortona, generously allowed us to photograph their corner of *paradiso.* We've shared many adventures with them and with Lee and Cecilia Cogher. To Gina and Mike Cerré, who brought Tuscany home on the Fine Living Channel, thank you. And to Nina Kotova and Barret Wissman and Daniel Wissman—friends and partners in the Tuscan Sun Music Festival—*salute.* Nina's cello concerto "Under the Tuscan Sun" is a joy forever. Toni Mirosevich and Shotsy Faust always welcomed us to Heaven House—*grazie mille.*

My eternal thanks to Peter Ginsberg, my agent, and Edwin Wintle of Curtis Brown, Ltd. I'm lucky to have Charlie Conrad as my editor. Working with Alana Watkins, Joanna Pinsker, Alison Presley, Rebecca Holland, Rebecca Cole, Maria Carella, Luisa Francavilla, Barbara Barthelmes at Broadway Books is a complete pleasure. To Steven Barclay of the Steven Barclay Agency—a big *grazie.* I am grateful to the editors of *Town & Country Travel* for publishing "*Pici*—Tuscan Soul Food" in their inaugural issue. A big thank you to Raphael Bemporad, an Italian gentleman, and Edward Sbragia and Lisa Klinck-Shea at Beringer Vineyards. Thank you, Carl Levine, for suggesting that we bring Tuscan furniture home. This led to our friendship with Jeff and Lynn Young, Michael Black, and Melanie Dunn at Drexel Heritage, Kate and Art Thompson at Laneventure, and to a grand venture for all of us. Monica Edwards and Steve Carlson have accompanied me on many jaunts with humor and skill. We are lucky to partner with Sferra Brothers, Wildwood Lamps, Miresco Rugs, and Vietri Ceramics—all Italophiles.

We thank Steven Rothfeld for his photographs, his enormous sensitivity as a traveller, and for the fun we had on the road and at home in Tuscany. Nancy Campana cheered us on from her bastion at Half Moon Bay and designed a book that thrilled us. Chef David Shalleck helped us cook for the Marin photograph sessions and made sure the plates looked beautiful. Giuseppina De Palma, our household goddess, did the same in Italy. Madeline Heinbockel, as always, helped me with organizing life and manuscripts. To Nancy Silverton, a bag of Bramasole plums anytime.

Our particular thanks to Il Sindaco Emanuele Rachini, mayor of Cortona, a man whose values protect the patrimony. I was graced by honorary citizenship of Arezzo and thank Il Sindaco Luigi Lucarini for that privilege. My gratitude to Barilla for the gala and the honor. Ed and I are most grateful to friends: Riccardo and Amy Bertocci, Donatella De Palma and Rupert Palmer, Vittoria and Giorgio Zappini, Eva Romina Fabianelli, Alessandra's baby Francesca Ludovici, Giuseppe Agnolucci, the entire Molesini family, Silvia Regi and Riccardo Baracchi, the Peruzzi clan, Lina Bartelli and Teodoro Manfreda, Lucio Ricci, Maria Petruccioli and Edo Perugini, Paolo Castelli, Santino and Massimo Cenci, Arnaldo Rossi, Emiliano Rossi and Ylenia Landucci, Stefano Cruscanti, Fabio Cenni, Paolo Pasquini, Leonardo Motolese, Andrea Alimenti, Roberto Fratoni and Nunziatina Picciafuochi, Bruno Bertocci, Fabrizio Brocchi, Giorgio and Lina Lamentini, Donatella Balducci and Isa Miretta Bennati. The Busatti family welcomes us with *prosecco*. They are gracious bearers of their long tradition of fabric making. Eugenio Lucani painted pure joy on our walls. Elio and Edoardo Capecchi literally moved the earth. Antonello Caprini brought the light and Claudio Cosci the water. Builders Danilo Cetica and Roberto Tanganelli restored Fonte delle Foglie to a new life.

To our great friends the Di Rosa family—Fulvio, Aurora, Patrito, and the princely Edoardo—immeasurable thanks. And, *per sempre,* our love to Fiorella, Placido, and Chiara Cardinali.

CONTENTS

AFTER DINNER
AT THE PANTE'S VILLA

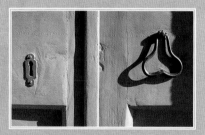

In 1990, we bought Bramasole, an abandoned, scorpion-inhabited, blackberry-choked villa perched on a terraced hillside just outside Cortona. My husband, Ed, and I were first known as "the French" (because we had a French license plate on our rented car). Later we were called the *stranieri,* the foreigners. We chose Tuscany for the serene landscape, the frescoes, the piazzas with their fountains and liveliness, the wine, the markets, the festas, and the perfect espresso. We stayed for the people and the way of life we learned from them. Now, after fourteen years of eating pasta al dente, we've found ourselves inextricably folded into the intense life of a small town. Without our permission, our private vacation and writing retreat became *home.*

Ten thousand joys attract us to life in Tuscany. Each time we push through the arrival doors at the Florence airport and speed toward Cortona, we both feel rushes of excitement as we pass toasted farmhouses surrounded by vineyards and, in the distance, silhouettes of walled villages. We still marvel: *a castle!* When we stop at an autostrada grill, Ed tastes his first espresso. Inevitably, he says, "At last, real coffee," and he thanks the *barista* as though he's been handed a gift. After that, he drives even faster. Just off the Valdichiana exit, we pass the tenth-century abbey of Farneta, our first marker that we're near home. I always look back to see the rounded brick apses, as Ed straightens out the curved roads through gentle fields of wheat and sunflowers. Climbing toward town, we love to see the golden stones, rippled tile roofs, and aqua dome of our little *città* nestled on the hillside. We stop at our gate. Bramasole looks mysteriously down on us, and we remember the first time we saw it, when I stepped through weeds taller than I, and said, jokingly, "This is it."

This is it. I didn't have the prescience to know that our lives were about to change profoundly and that we would become deeply married to this plot of land under the Medici fortress and the Etruscan wall. We live on the Strada della Memoria, where every cypress tree memorializes a Cortona boy killed in World War I. Six hundred local boys, what a horror. One of our current projects is replacing a hundred missing trees along the road. At night, with only moon and stars as light, these immense dark trees sentinel the road, and as I walk in the tide of cool currents that stream across the hills, I think what a good tribute the cypress trees are to those who forfeited the chance to live their full lives in this sublime landscape.

Entering the house after an absence brings back the first time I ever walked inside. The small rooms—so many of them and all the same size—were crammed with chests that provided homes for generations of mice and upright upholstered chairs that looked like Abraham Lincoln died there. Someone's bad attic. Lugubrious religious paintings hung over tubular iron beds. I was fascinated by the bleeding sacred hearts, the sappy Madonnas, and the saint—eyes rolled to heaven—with a dagger in her chest. I grew more excited by the minute. Stepping out on the balcony overlooking a classic Tuscan landscape, dotted with toffee-colored farms, I scarcely heard the agent's warning: *Signora, at any moment, please, the floor might collapse.*

Is it an homage to that initial impression that I, too, have my collection of religious paintings? Two Christs crowned with thorns, two Mary Magdalenes, several crucifixions, one Madonna and Child, and a few of the eye-rollers, too. I was stunned to open a gift from a friend and find a painting on tin of the saint with the dagger in her chest. The antique markets have stacks of these religious paintings, as well as other objects of fascination to a South Georgia Methodist. A visitor would view my bookcases as

a study in holy dismemberment, filled as they are with a collection of heads, arms, and legs of various saints and putti, but my collection of relics protects us (so far) from harm.

My study walls hold the studio portraits of an Italian family I have imagined for myself—a serene mother holding a letter (from whom?); a stray Fascist uncle all puffed up in his uniform; a cousin with scrolled curls and first communion white; a propped-up baby, his tiny penis proudly poking forward; and the sturdy grandmother of considerable girth, who looks as though she could tell off the butcher, stir the minestrone, and deliver twins all at once. The still life painting of cherries we found at an antique market, the iron bed we've dragged out of a junkyard near Olmo, and the chestnut *armadio* lugged up to the third floor—everything in our house reminds us of an adventure.

While I visit every room, Ed heads for the olive terraces. He knows each one of our original 160 olive trees by name. This year we bought a grove just below us, adding another 250 trees—more bottles of that liquid poetry, *olio d'oliva*. Ed named it Il Oliveto di Willie, Willie's olive grove, in hopes that someday our grandchild will continue the good work of husbanding a grove.

When we hand-label our oil for gifts to friends, we write, *organic, handpicked, unfiltered, extra virgin, cold-pressed by stone.* Extra virgin is oil with less than 1 percent acid, but we've learned to scoff at such a high bar. Ours, like other growers' oil in our area, has but a small fraction of 1 percent, so it is the virgin among all virgins. We bring it home from the mill and invite friends over for the tasting every year. By now, Ed simply scoops up a spoonful, while others of us dip in a finger, a piece of bread. This ritual links us to the deep taproot of Mediterranean life.

Another ritual is seed planting—always connected to the moon's phases. We're stunned to see our seeds sprouting, growing, flourishing so quickly in the ancient dirt. We, too, feel a rich connection to the land and the procession of the seasons. Our roots have spread. We have a tribe of Italian friends who put up with our version of Italian, and who show us, by example, the pleasure of living everyday life in this *bellissimo* landscape.

The first revelation from these friends—and the most influential—centers on home and friends and the table, the focus of celebration. Tuscans passionately love whatever plot of *terra* they live on and cultivate every inch with flowers and vegetables. They thrive on their local markets, which provide not only food but social life. Food, in Italy, is not cult but culture. In all my years in Italy, I've never once heard food connected to guilt. The pleasures of eating and drinking are never tortured into psychological struggles. The intense sense of community we feel in Cortona revolves around the table. *Mangiare bene, stare bene*—eat well, be well.

We hear constantly two Tuscan expressions, *per ora*, for now, and *per piacere*, as you please. These are links to why the Tuscans know how to live. After living so long in California, where being in the here and now is a mantra, in Italy I've finally absorbed *per ora*. You inquire about someone's health and they answer "Good, for now." That tacked-on phrase speaks to the realization that the moment is just that, and, almost superstitiously, we are wise to acknowledge the transitive nature of good fortune. *Per piacere* appears on menus—as you please. You can have whatever you want, the chef suggests. This carries over into daily exchanges. We relax into the laissez-faire attitudes of these anciently sophisticated people. Absorbing the resonances around these two concepts, our lives have changed. Friends drop by spontaneously for a chat. Just-picked wild asparagus translates instantly into an invitation to make a frittata with neighbors. A mention of a shop or Renaissance well or ruined *borgo* provokes an *"Andiamo"* response that appeals to me. We have learned to live by seasons and sun, rather than by the clock.

Once we were summer people. Now we just live here. Occasionally, when we go in a shop, the daughter calls to her father in the back, *"Babbo, i stranieri sono qui,"* "Daddy, the foreigners are here." But mostly we just glide in and about among all the others who are also lucky, by birth or choice, to have landed in such a place.

SILVIA REGI AT BRAMASOLE
NEXT PAGE BEFORE DINNER
AT THE PANTE'S VILLA

We live here. We also live in California, where we have family, a house and a garden, and twenty-five-years' worth of friendships. From the beginning, we began to bring Tuscany home. Pillows. *Parmigiano.* Stationery. Chocolate. Wine. Duvet covers. And, of course, shoes. Then we began to bring home something more lasting—a mind-set, a way of being in the world. Members of our family, who have established their own relationships with the Tuscan way of life, have done the same. Frequently, we talk about how living in Italy has changed our California home, our tables, what we pour in our glasses, the way we entertain—how we live our daily lives. Ed and I, working with our friend, photographer Steven Rothfeld, decided to explore this cultural symbiosis. Like our experience, his time in Tuscany has indelibly marked his California life.

Bringing Tuscany Home is an invitation. We document the portable aspects of Tuscany—practical advice and discoveries. But our intention is, as well, more sublime. This book is an invitation to a way of being, a guide to the good life, and a toast to the Tuscans, who inspire the world with their knowledge of how to live like the gods. We celebrate the spirit of friendship, the ease of living, and the sense of exuberance that we have found in this small hill town. Etruscan tombs from 800 B.C.E. show men and women reclining around the banquet table. We recognize the expression of contentment on their faces. The tradition is long. We have been fortunate to pick our strawberries, hang our sheets in the sun, sharpen our knives, pop open the local vino, light the candles, and slip into our places at the Tuscan feast.

CORTONA, EARLY MORNING

BRAMASOLE ON A FALL EVENING

La Casa Aperta

❈

THE OPEN HOUSE

La casa aperta, the open house—rain blows in the open windows, a visiting cat peers in the living room door, petals of bougainvillea land in the entrance hall, and the narcotizing scent of jasmine seeps from the upstairs terrace into the bedrooms. People come and go as naturally as the butterflies that drift by the mirrors. Those prime movers, our Cardinali neighbors, bring pickled eggplant, dried mushrooms, fruit cordials, and grappa. Chiara comes home from a week in Sardegna and surprises us with a *pensiero,* a thoughtful little gift of a shell necklace and a straw shopping bag. Beppe brings eggs, still with tiny feathers stuck to them. Lucio leaves yellow squash on the steps; Giusi arrives with *cenci,* fried "rags" of pastry; Giorgio brings wild boar. Among the Americans, a constant book exchange flows. How delicious to come home and find a nice stack of Marilyn's paperbacks on the wall. My neighbor, Melva, a fellow Californian, drops off apricot jam and home-baked bread. She hates the local salt-free bread we've grown accustomed to, and when I make toast from her bread I do too. I take a sack of green beans down to

CORTONA

Donatella and from the look in her eye, I understand that they, too, have more green beans than a human family can eat. The lovely musical-chair rhythm of giving and giving leaves no one standing alone.

When I started living at Bramasole, I had the intuition that the house was at home in the landscape and that by living here I would be at home too. My instinct proved true. The house—layered under an Etruscan wall, then a Medici fortress, and looking over the valley where Hannibal once pounced on the Romans—here my life changed, from the slightest detail of the quotidian to the large arcs of love and commitment. I daydream about each signora who lived in these rooms—where she shelled peas, rocked the grandchild, placed a vase of the pink roses that survived the thirty years of abandonment. I would like to share a pot of lemon balm tea with her on a winter afternoon while we cook a pot of black cabbage soup.

Now I would like to invite one of these women back to my house in California to show her how Bramasole travelled to America and took root, how the house opens to the breeze from the northern loop of the San Francisco Bay and to the sacred view of Mount Tamalpais, how the garden burgeons and the table magically expands. A pot of *ragù* is simmering. Ed is forming little pillows of gnocchi. My daughter has invited ten friends. The signora and I take a basket to the herb garden outside the kitchen. What music shall I play for her?

ONE OF MANY ROMAN ROADS
AROUND CORTONA

A wasp zooms through my study window and I see her land on the keyhole of my chest of drawers. She slips into the opening as simply as someone entering a pied-à-terre. From inside the drawer, I hear a muffled buzz. Minutes later, she pokes out her head, as if checking for traffic or rain, then takes off like an Alphajet. I already have spotted the mud huts she's building from daubs of dirt she carries. She lays her eggs inside each, then seals over the opening. The earthen domes in the back corner look like miniature Middle Eastern ruins on the edge of some desert. As of yet, I have not had the heart to scrape them out. But I do not want to put on a T-shirt and get stung under my arm by a mad baby wasp. All morning she keeps me company. I'm writing an article for a magazine; she's furthering her species. I am aware of her *being a wasp* but focused also on describing local trattorias.

Late in the afternoon, I'm still fact-checking. A bird flies in one window of my study and out the other. Even with a bird phobia that makes me gasp as it sweeps over my head, I'm actually charmed with this flyby. Part of my mind participates in the swallow's dip and angle. Smaller birds nest in cracks in the house's facade, along with bats. They never dive-bomb us as we eat at the table below, but I always fear they will. The ugly, just-hatched ones look out from a tiny triangular crack beside the guest room window. How cramped they must be, especially when Mama homes in with worms. Unconsciously, I flex my shoulders.

Ed calls me from the bathroom, where he is soaking his stone-bruised foot in the bidet. He has been distracted from an article he's reading in the *Times Literary Supplement* by two yellow jackets in mortal combat on the windowsill. They maneuver like TV wrestlers. One has torn the wings off the other, and I arrive in time to see the loser's head bitten off and carried aloft.

The garden's mercurial green lizards also go at each other ferociously. I wondered why so many lacked tails until I saw one writhing in agony while the friend, with

VIEW FROM HOTEL BELLOSGUARDO, FLORENCE

whom he had been sunning on the wall a few minutes previously, chomped on his back and pinned him down. He held his opponent with his feet and began to gnaw on the exact spot where the tail begins. I threw a glass of water on them and cooled their zeal fast. Mostly they dart about, enacting the expression *leapin' lizards,* flinging themselves over chasms between flowerpots the way a stunt driver in a car chase powers over a highway gap or a drawbridge. They charm me most when they crawl in and out of the birdhouse on the *cantina* windowsill, and when they sip from saucers under just-watered pots.

I love sharing the house and land with creatures. When the house is open, it follows that the mind creaks open, too. Beppe, who works with Ed on the land, is heartless toward porcupines. I'm fond of them even though they eat one bite out of a melon or tomato and move on to the next. He has surrounded the garden with wire fencing, dug down a foot into the ground. He also set a trap, and I pray the porcupines do not enter that fatal door. Our neighbor would have them for pasta sauce. On nights of insomnia, I picture the porcupine nosing into the earth around the fence, dropping quills in the chard, inching through a small gap at the post and scurrying toward the melons. I have seen a pair of them crossing the rose garden in the moonlight, their fans of erect quills gleaming.

Now a bee zooms in, drinks from the faucet, and flies out. During lavender season, yellow, orange, blue, and white butterflies drift through the bedroom and light on my black shirt drying on a chair. One winter an owl found a way into the attic and, in the hour of dawn, we heard him flying among the beams. As spring came, Placido discovered an owlet on our hillside, one-hand high and covered with gossamer feathers the color of smoke. For a few weeks, the owl sat on the back of a chair next to Placido while we had dinner. He would hop on your hand—not my hand, no thanks—and nibble a piece of *parmigiano.* Though he seemed otherworldly, with his swivel head and foil-backed eyes, we named him Allocco, which is a

MONASTIC ENTRANCE TO FRANCES AND ED'S CALIFORNIA HOME

kind of owl but also a fool, a clown. He began to spread his wings and flap. Someone accidentally left the cage open one night, and Allocco was gone the next morning. Sometimes when an owl hoots from the pine trees, we call back "Ciao, Allocco." I can still feel those feathers, closer to fur than feathers, and see his flat-eyed look full of an expectation we had no way to meet.

This Möbius inside/outside seamlessness began to change my way of experiencing the world from about five minutes after I first walked through the *portone,* the big front door of Bramasole. As a liberal arts academic for twenty-three years, in the heady theoretical era of deconstruction and intensely abstracted critical theory, I'd imbibed too often the idea that experience came to one through language structures wide open to interpretation but nonetheless laid like railroad tracks across the DNA. Language created experience but language was endlessly mutable. With all interpretation suspect, the author became a hapless maker of kaleidoscopic word patterns. We were awash in relativism. In America, I found that my life was influenced too strongly by cultural currents; in Italy, the influence was coming more from the spirit of place. One of my university colleagues, I recall, said nature was "freaky and boring." Anything that was not a cultural construct was irrelevant. This time of talking heads was, for many, exhilarating; for me, exasperating. My colleague Steve and I closed his office door against the seeping gas of meaninglessness in our chosen fields. He poured espresso into the little cups I brought home from Italy and we talked about Eugène Atget's photographs, French salt, opera, and the unfashionable, highly individual authors we loved.

Away from work, I'd go for weeks with my feet touching no earth. But even in San Francisco, where I lived, raccoons made their way up three flights of back stairs and crawled through Sister's cat door. I was thrilled to come home and find three of them in the middle of the kitchen floor eating my five-pound bar of cooking chocolate. When Ed shooed them out with a broom, I watched them waddle down the steps in a

huff. Reluctantly they returned to their storm drains, and Sister, black fur electrified, emerged from hiding in a closet. When we heard the raccoons were dangerous, we bought an electronic collar for Sister. With her own cat door opener, only she could nose the little plastic flap and enter the premises.

Nights in our kitchen were scented by jasmine that had bolted up the three flights and draped the back porch with languorous sweetness. The herbs in my window box leaned valiantly into the wind and sparingly offered me leaves of thyme and oregano. Even on the cold nights, I slept with the window open so I could hear the mournful foghorns on the bay, could conjure people on the decks of boats with the slap of salt wind on their faces, the lights of the city appearing and disappearing in the roiling waves of fog.

The Victorian flat often swayed in small earthquakes, creaking like a ship. The bowed windows fore and aft, east and west, seemed perpetually pointing toward a destination we might sail to through the fog. Across the street my neighbor put his head down on his desk. *Am I looking in a mirror?* Was he weeping or taking a nap? I never knew but checked on him till he sat up, walked to his kitchen, and stared into the fridge. A few times a rogue flock of brilliant green parrots landed on the telephone wire between the two houses. My neighbor slouched in front of the TV, a giant Pepsi balanced on his stomach. I wanted to shout, "Get up! Look out your window. Parrots in the city! It's straight out of Márquez. Take it as a sign."

Later, I recognized all the longing I'd had in the city for a life connected with the natural world. In San Francisco, my house was a haven, an enclave, a retreat from work. In Tuscany, those words don't come to mind, although they're still true. Maybe I think of home differently because I need less respite from my life. Or maybe Bramasole found me ready to fling open the doors.

A few years in Tuscany and I have developed my own philosophy, which began that first summer when I'd lie in bed at night and hear thousands of bees in the

linden flowers. The collective hum made me feel that I was inside a hive, a drowsy queen in the dark. At dawn, the sun hoisting itself over the mountains smeared the walls with glistening, honey-colored light. Feeling or thought, I wondered at that moment. *Both,* I knew. The big collision of the two makes experience spectacular. My academic colleagues' heavy cloud of theory evaporated. I began to breathe easily among the ancient absolutes.

Direct and primitive contact with mud huts of wasps and scattered bougainvillea petals takes me way back somewhere before language. Then leads me freshly back to language. Not only a matter of apertures, my open-house philosophy lines up with the phenomenologists, whose focus is on *essence.* Edmund Husserl, one of the founders of phenomenology, emphasized *Zu den Sachen selbst,* immediate experience of the thing itself, without presuppositions or preconceptions. Before living here, I would have doubted Husserl—isn't it impossible to escape subjectivity and reality-as-we-know-it? Doesn't all experience involve prejudgments lodged in the brain by tradition, inheritance, and belief? Isn't everything simply out there in the world, to be seen or not?

Noumenon, a word poets love to use: the thing or event existing in its own light. The *concept* so distant from the pouf of the lips pronouncing the soft vowels, from the *experience* of the word *lavender* as I sit by the actual lavender at the front door. In the heat, a mauve haze seems to rise with the scent. Bees and butterflies swirl and burrow. The bees are burly and rotund. Their patterns of flight and those of the butterflies—all light and color—coexist within the hard rhythm of cicadas in the linden trees. The mind empties, or rather, opens to the silence of the black and white butterfly whose wings pray, then lift to fly to the next blossom, and to the cozy bumble of the furry bee. The phenomenologists wrote of "bracketing" experience, framing it as through a lens, and attending to it thoughtfully. The result is a synesthesia

with the world as it comes to us, instead of the way we preconceive or theorize it. The bee, the cicada, the butterfly, the amethyst-colored scent, exist together intensely for a few moments. And, me? I'm not even here.

My house: the perceiving, unthinking, wordless mind expanding. This is the heart of all my experiences of living in Tuscany. The open house became a way of life.

On sweltering July afternoons, we rest in bed with the fan directed our way. I have a new novel to read, and Ed is instantly asleep after his morning with the stonemasons and blacksmith. The cicadas—metabolic sound of childhood in the South, and now the signal of high summer in Tuscany—twang in the linden trees. My early memories of summer have this background chorus, this two-note repetition that becomes a monotonous, soothing raga. Ravi Shankar has landed in a tree with his sitar.

To my own memories, a friend's experience has annealed. When the cicadas hatched this year, I remarked to Fulvio that they were louder in Greece than here. "Yes, the cicadas. I was in Greece when I was nineteen—with my girlfriend. I always remember floating in the warm Aegean and hearing them on the island. Beautiful." So I lie in bed thinking of the lithe young body buoyant in a warm sea and this bacchic chorus filling the air. This blends with the memory of Lawrence Durrell's *Prospero's Cell.* Newly arrived on a Greek island, the young writer, just discovering his talent, describes throwing cherries in the clear sea. His wife swims down to the sandy bottom and brings them up in her teeth.

My novel holds me for five pages and I start to doze. The intense sun bleaches the landscape. I turn the pillow over to the cool side, read again, and fall into a space where I imagine that our distant and dormant volcano, Monte Amiata, erupts and we are suddenly drowned in lava, as were the people in Pompeii, going about their

HOTEL VILLA BALDELLI, CORTONA

breadmaking, money-changing, bathing; their bodies at once extinguished and immortalized. Our own tableau, a thousand years hence, would include the ice pack in an old linen towel wrapped around Ed's foot. Would include the white curtains on our painted iron bed and four apricot roses in an antique glass bottle. These dream-soaked afternoons with the leisure of a book, a fan, a down pillow . . . Crack open the cooled lava and find our remnants of happiness.

ED SUNNING IN WILLIE'S OLIVE GROVE

{29}

BRINGING TUSCANY HOME

NANCY SILVERTON'S ITALIAN PLUM TART

Nancy has restored a house in Panicale. Aromas drifting out her kitchen window must make the neighbors wildly hungry. Nancy started La Brea Bakery in Los Angeles and owns Campanile restaurant, in addition to writing books on baking. When we went over to admire her new ochre walls, she served this tart.

1 RECIPE SWEET PASTRY DOUGH (SEE RECIPE BELOW)
2 POUNDS ITALIAN PRUNE PLUMS, PITTED AND QUARTERED
1 EGG
⅓ CUP GRANULATED SUGAR
3½ TABLESPOONS ALL-PURPOSE FLOUR, SIFTED
½ STICK (2 OUNCES) UNSALTED BUTTER
1 VANILLA BEAN, SPLIT AND SCRAPED
2 TEASPOONS ALMOND EXTRACT
6 TABLESPOONS ALMOND MEAL (BLANCHED AND FINELY GROUND ALMONDS)

✸ Preheat the oven to 350°F. Adjust rack to middle position.

✸ Roll out the sweet pastry dough on a lightly floured surface to a thickness of ⅛ to ¼ inch. Butter a 10-x-1-inch flan ring and line it with the dough.

✸ Whisk together the egg and sugar until combined. Beat in the flour until well mixed. Set aside.

✸ In a small saucepan, heat the butter and vanilla bean over high heat until brown and foamy. Continue heating until the bubbles subside and the butter is dark brown and smoking and gives off a nutty aroma. Whisking continuously, pour the hot butter in a steady stream into the egg mixture, combining well. Remove the vanilla bean. Stir in the almond extract and almond meal, mixing well.

✸ Spread the brown butter mixture evenly over the bottom of the tart shell, using the back of a spoon or an offset spatula. Starting at the outside edge of the shell, place the plums on their sides in concentric circles, completely covering the surface. Arrange a few pieces in the center to fill in the gaps.

✸ Bake for 50 to 60 minutes, until the crust is light brown and the filling is almost set. The tart will seem a bit juicy when you take it out of the oven, but it will firm up as it cools. When cool, slip a cardboard round underneath and remove the flan ring.

SWEET PASTRY DOUGH

1 CUP PLUS 6 TABLESPOONS UNBLEACHED PASTRY FLOUR OR UNBLEACHED ALL-PURPOSE FLOUR
¼ CUP GRANULATED SUGAR
1 STICK (4 OUNCES) UNSALTED BUTTER, CUT INTO ½-INCH CUBES AND FROZEN
1 EXTRA-LARGE EGG YOLK
2 TABLESPOONS HEAVY CREAM

✸ In a food processor with steel blade or mixer bowl fitted with a paddle, combine flour and sugar and pulse or mix on low. Add the butter and pulse on and off, or mix on low, until the dough barely comes together.

✸ In a small bowl, whisk together the egg yolk and cream. Add the butter mixture and pulse a few times or mix on low until the dough barely comes together.

✸ Turn the dough out onto a lightly floured work surface. Dip the heel of your hand in flour and, working with small sections, smear the dough away from you to blend it. When the dough has been all smeared out, using a metal scraper or spatula, scrape and gather it to-gether. Gently knead and gather into a ball. Flatten into a disk, wrap in plastic, and chill at least 2 hours, until firm.

SERVES 8 TO 10

AT THE MAYES HOME IN CALIFORNIA

Le Stanze

THE ROOMS

Tuscan country houses look as though they were formed by the landscape itself rather than by the human hand. They are remarkable for their bold simplicity. From town to town, the houses' stone color varies from gray to sand to gold, but architecturally the houses share similar characteristics. The window surrounds usually are *pietra serena,* that most-admired blue-gray stone. Shutters allow you to batten the hatches in storms and to close out the heat in the depth of summer. In many farmhouses, an outside stair-case rises to the second floor, where the family lived. The animals were kept below. Those lower quarters have arched openings for carts, if the family had oxen. When such houses are remodeled, these become graceful doors opening to the outside. Some lovers of rusticity retain the wooden mangers along the back walls as book racks or display space for vintage farm tools or cooking equipment. Small villas, such as Bramasole, often had a closed-off apartment for the resident farm family, and the large villas had numerous separate houses for the workers. The oldest farms and the grandest Medici villas retain the

FRANCES'S "ROOM OF ONE'S OWN"
AT BRAMASOLE

CALIFORNIA MEYER LEMONS IN
FRANCES'S MARIN DINING ROOM

DETAILS FROM WALL PAINTINGS
BY EUGENIO LUCANI AT
IL FALCONIERE, CORTONA

ghost of the heavy-bottomed fortress architecture, even if more windows were added later and the watchtowers were turned into clock towers or lopped off and recycled as rooms. The solid structures reinforce the idea of the house as a stronghold.

I admire the thickness of the walls in these houses, the plaster, like birthday-cake icing, and the mellow brick floors. Their *cantinas* store the year's wine in corked, green-glass demijohns, which are now being replaced by *fustini*, soulless stainless-steel tanks. Often, by trash receptacles, we spot three or four demijohns, still in their old straw casing, and jump out of the car to grab them quickly, before any of our neighbors can see us taking "trash." My friend Donatella collects these demijohns and places them all over her garden.

Also from the *cantina*, I love the terra-cotta olive oil jars, which are now used to stash umbrellas and walking sticks. No old farmhouse lacks an enormous fireplace, used not only for cooking but as the place where family and friends gathered to sip grappa and talk. Some fireplaces are so large that they accommodate a couple of crude, rush-bottomed chairs inside. You sit there if you really want to feel toasty.

❦

I have always been enchanted (my daughter would say obsessed) with houses. My first ones were wooden lawn chairs tipped together, a shoebox for a stove—the burners drawn in crayon—and a grassy nest for dolls. When I was ten, I was allowed to select the colors and fabrics for my room. I chose dark brown walls and a green-and-brown chintz print for the beds and curtains. I have never since been able to stand those colors, even for a pair of socks. In college in Florida, my roommate Rena and I painted our apartment lavender with bunches of grapes in the corners of the ceiling. We bought cotton rugs at an outlet and hung the walls with Picasso posters and paintings by Rena's mother. Brahms's "Academic Festival Overture" was our favorite record, and we played it at maximum volume while we sat under those portable hair dryers with thick shower-cap hoods stretched over wire-brush rollers. We outlined our lips with tiny brushes slashed through lipstick then dipped in pomegranate-scented gloss. The exuberance of the chorus booming out Latin *gaudeamus igitur* exhilarated us.

Our passes at domestic life were limited to meatloaf and fish sticks, although we invited dates for Thanksgiving and burned the turkey on the outside while the inside remained raw. Someone discovered the little melted plastic bag of innards while searching in vain for stuffing. My grandfather had given me his old Oldsmobile and we often drove it through the In-N-Out Burger, turned up the air, and floor-boarded it out to Paine's Prairie, where we sat on a knoll with our greasy sack. Hundreds of snakes sought the high ground of the road after a rain, the vibrant, deadly coral snakes, as well as common water moccasins and rattlers. Sometimes we saw great alligators with horrifying open mouths lumbering toward a sinkhole of water. Odd, we both felt at home there. We'd left the fine and sedate women's college in Virginia. We wanted adventure. By the time we'd decided to transfer, the university dorms and sorority houses were full. We were forced to find an apartment, though our parents were dubious. After the isolation of the women's college, we went out on dates every night for a year. Rena met a grad student she later married, but I reveled in changing boyfriends every few weeks. We had not got wind of the sexual freedom to come late in the sixties and neither of us ever dreamed of a date staying over.

AT THE PANTE'S VILLA
CAPPUCCINI

A few years in my life I would like to have in a bottle. From that year I'd pour out joy and freedom. We had ferns and music—we also loved the Soviet Army Chorus—and poetry books and sunlight reaching all the corners of the rooms.

All those elements have remained for me the essentials of a house. The place, too, moved into me. Florida—balmy, embracing air, Spanish moss swaying in the oaks along the street, sidewalks crowded with bridal wreath and tea olive, screened porches banked by tree-sized azaleas, and the flat, flat land baking under a southern sun. I could move there tomorrow.

When I married and moved into graduate student housing in California, my friends were making bookcases from bricks and boards. Their sofas were Salvation Army day beds covered with Indian bedspreads and pillows. Pillows everywhere. I already had inherited the family passion for fabrics. Since my great-grandfather, grandfather, and father were in the cotton mill business, I hardly could escape. I sewed yards of cheap gauze fabric into airy curtains. I made striped pull-down shades. I spent weekends at used furniture stores around Stanford, and later at country auctions around Princeton. My $35 Sheraton sofa had a good seventy-five years on it. I went over my preset limit and came home with a French trumeau, a foxed mirror topped by

FAR LEFT BEDROOM AT THE MAYES HOUSE: FRESCO COLORS, WITH MOUNT TAMALPAIS IN THE DISTANCE **LEFT** THE MIRROR FOUND IN VENICE **RIGHT** FROSTED WATERMELON ARMLESS CHAIR

a Fragonard-style painting. I bought a brass bed for $2 and a bergère for $40. I still have most of the things I bought as a twenty-four-year-old. Since we were living on scholarships—they were more generous then—I did a lot of stripping and painting. It never occurred to me that I could not live in a beautiful apartment just because of a lack of money.

In my adult life I have always preferred old houses. In the East, I lived in two pre-Revolutionary War houses with great spirit. They guided me toward preferences for highboys, Chippendale, and important chinoiserie dining-room chairs in Queen Anne style, painted and lacquered. The houses yielded secrets—pre-Revolutionary postage stamps beneath layers of milk paint on a cupboard door, penciled inscriptions in the attic, medicine bottles in the herb garden dirt, a peony hedge that rose and graced the front yard with its lipstick-kissed pink blossoms. I found a ledger recording that the millwright had nailed together a coffin for a neighbor's child. A house with a history appealed to me strongly. With the houses came, again, that connection to a sense of place. In Bedford, Massachusetts, and later in Somers, New York, I felt the closeness of history. Looking out at the small park in front of our house, I could almost see the Minutemen rallying, as they had on April 19, 1775, and Paul Revere thundering by on his way to Concord. In both places, the houses were among others of similar age. In the snow or rain, time dissolved. In the emptied street, horse-drawn carriages might round the curve, bread might be baking in the fireplace's brick oven, the mysterious Delicy, who wrote on the attic walls, might descend the stair.

Years in California and in Tuscany never have erased the languid pleasure of Florida air—no night feels as sweet as a southern summer night in May. *My place,* the body feels. And the polar opposite but also powerful New England atmosphere— the profound comfort of a lilac hedge, lamplight falling from windows onto billowing snow, a fanlight reflecting a million wavy yellow leaves in fall. Although I am a person who expected to be rooted in one spot forever, as it has turned out I love having the memories of living in many places.

⌖

After settling part-time in Tuscany, I've been amazed at the fast-forward evolution of my preferences about where to live. I fell hard for the highly codified Tuscan style, as well as the local way of life. After I sold my San Francisco Victorian flat, I moved for three years to the western part of the city because I wanted to live nearer the sea. Tuscany had so changed my preferences for living that I longed for a Mediterranean-style house. The one I found had graceful arches and balconies, French doors, and large windows to let in the ocean light. But the stucco exterior was dirty white. The yard looked disgraceful, landscaped in the twenties and neglected for untold years. Immediately, I changed the color to apricot, planted lemon trees, bricked the patio, and installed a fountain. Even before the first plant, the Tuscan garden had a fountain. I planted Carolina jasmine and clematis and trailing geraniums everywhere. From my upstairs bedroom in the California-Spanish house, I saw the Pacific horizon, sailboats, and splendid, brazen sunsets. The foggy mornings were mystical. But Italy's climate had spoiled us for the sun. After only three years—one devoted to remodeling—we, on impulse, looked at houses in Marin, just north of the Golden Gate.

For the first time in my life, we now live in a new house. It, too, is Mediterranean—this is now a strong preference. The house was beige when we moved in. Where is it written that houses might be beige? Any dun-colored house would look better if painted pineapple, cream, ochre, or even a smart sage. I had ours painted the same apricot as the San Francisco house, transforming it from a drab, looming hulk to a place that said *home.* What drew me most was a feeling of spareness, almost an austerity to the long hallway that the rooms abut. It reminded me of Romanesque cloisters and I thought I might feel a holy peace as I walked there.

That quality also reminded me of Tuscan houses with their large silences. A round fountain in the middle of the driveway looked a little mafioso to me at first, but I've grown to like it. Tuscan colors feel at home inside too. Shades of peach and yellow remind me every day of a Tuscan dawn.

The joys of a new (five-year-old) house are bigger closets, kitchens with work space, luxurious, even sybaritic, bathrooms. I have memories of old houses and plenty of history in Tuscany to keep me positioned in time. The other pleasure of a new house is its tabula rasa aspect. I can import my permeable indoor/outdoor Tuscan life and the place absorbs it. In warm weather, the doors are open. Trumpet vines on a trellis soften the garage, that ugliest of twentieth-century additions to domestic architecture. I've always hated a big garage that faces out, looking more important to the eye than the rest of the house. At my house, however, if they'd put the garage on the side, you'd drive off a cliff. The disguise of climbing vines will have to do. Enormous pots of Meyer lemons, surrounded by lavender, make the front porch welcoming. Besides their ornamental value, the sweet variety of citrus makes fantastic preserved lemons. Outside the kitchen, I planted fourteen varieties of thyme and a ring of chives around a stone birdbath. Several types of mint thrive in a large Tuscan pot. Rosemary sprawls along the back of the house. Basil and oregano under spiraling wire domes escape the jaws of marauding deer, who ignore my other herbs but fancy these.

Soon after we bought the house, we returned to Italy to celebrate Ed's fiftieth birthday in Venice. Wandering on the island of Murano, we found an outlandish mirror. Maybe every house has one defining object around which all the rest of the house radiates. During most incarnations in my life, I would have walked right by that mirror, but this time, I stopped and wondered how many years it had reflected the watery lagoon, how many fascinating Venetian faces had gazed into it. The froufrou pinkish flowers popping out from the glass frame and the heraldic silhouettes of Napoleonic soldiers and the curly edges were just too much. "It's like a piece of music," Ed said, "music turned to glass. Air on a something-string . . ." The store owner showed us how the little decorative pieces all came off neatly.

"Everything is so fragile," I said.

"*Signora, no problema.*" We responded to his warm smile and hint of spicy cologne. His name, Renato Schiavon, intrigued me because *schiavo* means "slave." (The root of the salutation *ciao* also comes from *schiavo*, and once meant "your slave," as in the phrase, "at your service.") With a dark name conjuring the interstices of Venetian trading, he seemed to embody all the convoluted history of that watery republic. He'd taken us immediately away from the new—to my eye, gaudy—mirrors and chandeliers. Upstairs, he kept older treasures. Instead of the hard-candy colors we'd seen in most of the shops, the glass colors on his old mirror frames were fluid. The pink frame of my mirror is like iced rosé; the flower stems are the color of lemonade.

The mirror arrived in California encased in a wooden crate packed with wet straw. The doges must have shipped their loot back to Venice the same way. The stemmed flowers that dance out around the mirror were wound with bubble wrap. Not a crack. This shipment was a revelation because it convinced me that *anything* could be shipped. After all, those old robber barons took apart whole monasteries and shipped them back to America. Our California house now happily lives with other Italian treasures—a painted eighteenth-century *armadio*, chest, bed, desk and tables, enormous old bookcases, lamps, and paintings. Compared to U.S. prices—there's no comparison. Europe, despite thousands of American dealers raiding every conceivable corner, still is full of affordable treasures. Shipping is worth the trouble. When our shipments arrive, it seems miraculous that the marble sink and blue-gray bookcase we bought at the Cortona antique market now stand in our driveway.

TROMPE L'OEIL WINDOW AT
VILLA LA GAMBERAIA

STONES ON DUOMO CAMPANILE,
FLORENCE

LUCANI BAR AT VILLA MARSILI

Friends who visit us in Tuscany sometimes leave their purchases from the Arezzo antique market—a console, display case, chairs—to be included in our next shipment, so they're dropping by as the crates are unpacked. We send small and large containers by air and sea. One shipment journeyed from Cortona to Genoa to Rotterdam to Houston, then by train to Los Angeles and by truck to the Bay Area. Nothing, so far, has been damaged, except the base of a lamp. The shippers build such solid *case, houses,* that we hate to throw them away. Ed gets out his drill and unwinds fifty or so screws from each box and the drivers hoist things into the house. The hard part is knowing precisely where something is going. Ed keeps saying, "Are you sure? Is it too wide?" After the shippers leave, he hates to see me, head cocked, regarding the *armadio,* back-breaking to move, that really would work better upstairs.

I saw right away that what I was bringing back to my California house was *color.* From the instant I'd stepped out of the car in front of Bramasole and looked up at the smeared rose, sienna, and apricot facade, a new love of color started to ride my

brain waves. I think the fresco colors of Masaccio, Piero della Francesca, and Perugino—soft but vivid—are easy to live with and provide stimulation and comfort. Color continues to delight me in Italy: a coved coral ceiling in Rome, a pocked antique-blue wall, Aurora's saffron sweater, the neon orange hair of the Annunciation angel in Fra Angelico's painting, Fulvio's pale cooking-apple-green kitchen walls, our Mediterranean-blue Alfa, violet shadows in folds of hills, dusty leaves of caper plants

OUTDOOR TABLE,
IL FALCONIERE

against a stone wall, the verdigris and peach dome of Santa Maria Novella, quicksilver olive leaves twirling in the sunlight, waxy citrus blossoms and lemons shining in the moonlight, a saint's creamy marble dress rippled with rose by sun through stained glass.

As Bramasole evolved, we experimented more with painted borders and not-white rooms. Although whitewashed plaster over stone is traditional, the Tuscans also love their painted, fanciful door frames and fresco-type murals, which are often landscapes but sometimes barnyard scenes or balconies draped with flowers. We found in the dining room a wonderful fresco. (I described the accidental discovery in *Under the Tuscan Sun*.) Italians take such discoveries for granted. So much so that the plumber wrote his boss's telephone number right on the sky. Although we were outraged at the time, we've found that the plumber's number comes in handy. Under the whitewash of an upstairs bedroom, we found foot-wide marine-blue and white stripes. My daughter replicated that idea in California for her baby's nursery, adding a blue flying elephant to hang from the ceiling.

Looking at everything from stone farmhouses to grand palazzos, I responded to the sense of spareness, almost an austerity, that felt clean and spacious. But at the same time, the Tuscan tradition I was uncovering also deeply involved a sense of play.

We painted Ed's study and the adjoining bedroom at Bramasole the same green as the new olive oil, since Ed's passion centers on olives. He loves our surviving remnants of a vineyard as well. I designed a pattern of grapes and leaves, and our friends Antonio and Patrizia made stencils, then painted wide borders in both rooms. They'd previously painted an Etruscan wave border in the original bathroom of the house. A few months after we moved to Bramasole, our friend Shera visited and painted over the main guest room windows arcs of scumbled blue with gold Giotto stars scattered in those little skies.

We moved into a new realm when we met Eugenio Lucani. Legendary in our area, he is a self-taught decorative painter. I love his name. Lucani connects directly to the ancient *lucani* people of southern Italy and also recalls to me the local Etruscans—their rulers were *lucumone*. His first name has *genius* lurking in it. We'd admired his whimsical landscapes behind trompe l'oeil balustrades in several villas, and at our friends' hotel, Il Falconiere, many of his borders and birds and pergolas grace the walls. Locally, when you remark on something extraordinary painted on a wall, the owner usually will say with obvious pride, "Lucani."

Eugenio is a compact, slender man with a sculptured face lighted by the fire of his ardor for painting. I love his blue eyes. They seem to reflect all the skies he has painted in his long life. He was always drawing as a boy before World War II. After the war, he was a young man in a place with no demand for what he desired to do. Italy was re-building, and only gradually, gradually he began to work at his art. He is the kind of artist I admire most, a sui generis artist whose love always has propelled him. He is of the place, and the place made him. He admires Perugino, the artist from just over the hills, Fra Angelico, who worked for fourteen years in Cortona, and, of course, Michelangelo. He has painted chapels with religious scenes, large landscapes, neoclassi-cal panels, and dozens of fruit garlands and borders. His wit shines. A painted door with an open book on the threshold opens to a landscape. A real mirror is held by a painted frame. A cat sits on the pedestal of a gazebo. Over the years, Eugenio has acted in forty-five comedies with the local theater troupe. The attraction is clear.

Many of the rooms at Bramasole are white. When he came to our house, it almost seemed that the white hurt his eyes. *"Bianco è spento,"* he said, not unkindly. White is lifeless.

"But the white keeps cool in the hot summers, and also objects stand out against white walls." I gestured at a black iron cross I found at an antique market.

LUCANI PAINTING IN FRANCES'S STUDY
RIGHT MORE LUCANI DETAILS

"*Freddo,*" he said. Cold. He looked in at the painted effects we have in several rooms. "*Non c'è male,*" he acknowledged. Not bad. We drove in his Fiat—he drives fast and with enormous confidence—to his house and looked through two books recording the work he's done.

"What is your favorite work?" I ask. He points out the Pompeiian-style geometric grotesques that adorn ceilings and walls in several of his works.

"Something different," he explains.

Back at our house, we walked through the rooms. I showed him an album of wildflower photographs I kept one wet spring when the terraces sent forth every bloom known to Tuscany. We began to talk about a wildflower border in my yellow study and its adjoining reading room. I especially like ephemeral dog roses because as a child I looked for them along country roads in Georgia, where they're called Cherokee roses. The next week Eugenio arrived with his assistant, Marino Pazzagli, and we cleared the reading room for wheeled scaffolding. They set to work, sketching the leaves and canes with pencil. I requested local birds, especially the glorious *upupa,* hoopoe. By the end of the second day, the fragile pink roses were blooming on my walls. When I came home the next day, two hoopoes had settled on a branch, and on other walls, a yellow finch, a pair of swallows, and a blackbird. He added a dragonfly. Then he moved to the adjoining room, my study, where he painted a rhythmic border of the *convolvulus,* the wild morning glory. Because we have so much lavender, our garden attracts thousands of butterflies in summer. I told Eugenio this and then found a dozen of them flitting among his flowers. He allowed a bee to settle on one leaf and a green beetle on another. Now when I write in my study, his vine charms me. A room painted with such joy imparts more joy.

Eugenio's main interest was our third-floor stairwell wall, a tall blank space just asking for him. It even has three pediments he can incorporate into his design. We talked about his landscapes. I admired the serene hills he painted in the Bar Vanelli in

Camucia. I told him we love the olive harvest. A scene started to take shape in my mind—an olive grove on terraced hills, with figures spreading nets, strapping on their baskets, and climbing into the branches. He became quiet and just looked. I decided to let him do what he wanted. As I am writing this, he is on scaffolding at Bramasole. I'm imagining the colors, the design, his intent face as he works. The rest of the stairwell walls will have to be repainted when he finishes, so the color will meld seamlessly with his work. No going back now to cold white.

Because of the years of living in Tuscany, my preferences for what to bring into my rooms has changed entirely too. I liked learning that the Italian word for room is *stanza*. As a poet, this appealed to me as I looked at Bramasole's walls, blank as pieces of paper. A poem involves a sense of care about lines and words, but a poem's source comes from an instinct toward a subject. Not what to say about a subject but how to approach the essence of the subject. My instinct for poetry transferred something to my ideas of how I wanted the rooms to *be*—not look, exactly, but how I wanted to feel when I was in them. I began to dream of how the rooms in my house would reflect our new life on that hillside.

I immediately started going to local shops and antique markets. I found two curvaceous iron beds in a junkyard and had Egisto, the blacksmith, blast off the rust. I found good shops, whose owners became friends. One day I spotted a dressing table with a mirror supported by carved dolphins in a Cortona store. For the first time in my life I wanted to powder my nose.

Anselmo, our real estate agent, who later became both our gardener and friend, took me to dusty hay barns and great aunts' houses, where the pasta is still rolled out daily on the marble-topped kitchen table, which has a hole on the side where the rolling pin fits. Out of my fascination with Tuscan houses, I went with him to look at property coming up for sale. He careened around curves on unpaved roads. The car

briefly sailed when he hit a bump, then banged down onto the rocky roadbed. Usually the owner was an ancient woman who no longer could manage and had decided most reluctantly to sell. The women all were tiny, with apple-doll faces and black dresses. I remember the tears, the photo of the dead husband in his wedding suit, the conclusive, *"La vita è così,"* Life is like that, and the tours through the spare, immaculate rooms with white crocheted curtains and woven white bedspreads that did not conceal the two dips made by tired bodies, and I remember most of all the feel of the women's hands. Each would take my hand in her smaller, cool, dry, hard hand, squeezing tight, uncomfortably so, reminding me of crossing streets in Macon with my mother, whose grip in the unfamiliar traffic left the imprints of my birthstone ring on the sides of my fingers. The clean, austere rooms exuded a monastic peace. Our visits involved long talks in the kitchen, with the ubiquitous bottle of homemade *vin santo* brought out of the cantina and the tooth-cracking biscotti served. Anselmo, lacking the sales instinct, sipped his *vin santo* and looked concerned. For me, this comprised a course in Tuscan Vernacular Interiors 101. I absorbed slowly an awareness of the timeless quality of the rooms. No trends, no fashion—just a sense of comfortable continuation in history. I also fell into a time warp, bending me back to the Middle Ages, except for the TV droning in the kitchen. Chickens scattered as Anselmo's big Alfa roared out of the yards. I was speechless as time unwarped and deposited me in the present tense again. "Do you know what *minimalism* is?" I asked Anselmo.

"Is that some idea that less is less?"

"Well, yes. Her house has kind of an antique minimalism decor."

He drove on.

EARLY MORNING IN THE
TUSCAN COUNTRYSIDE

All these deep-country houses had a *madia,* a sturdy chestnut dresser the top of which opens for the storage of rising bread. Now a *madia* often has a more fashionable use. Left open, it's a good place to keep grappa and other liqueurs. Some restaurants pile them with loaves of bread. The old kitchens also had single-stone sinks that drained directly out into the yard through a mouse-sized hole in the back. Every house I saw had iron beds and a cross on the wall over each. In spring, the parish priest still comes by to bless every room of the house. The olive branch he brings inevitably gets tucked behind one of the crosses, where it remains until brittle with dust.

At Bramasole, the challenge of the house is its small rooms. There are many of them—fourteen. Since home is seven thousand miles away, I have no temptation to bring castoffs from my garage and attic.

The first exciting discovery was a dining-room table in Fabrizio's *magazzino,* storeroom. Fabrizio is a young dealer who has a talent for refinishing. Mention a few pieces you need, and soon the *telefonino* is ringing. We're looking for a round table, I told him. Instead, he found an oval walnut table where ten can gather for great bowls of *ribollita,* as they have for generations. Soon after, across the valley in Monte San Savino, I found a cabinet with wavy glass doors, perfectly scaled to my small dining room. The cups and plates stacked inside remind me of thousands of birthday dinners with the platter taken down for long-roasted lamb.

I've discovered the pleasure of having furniture made, for this house as well as my house in California. It's fun to work with local artists on paint finishes and decoration. One lives across the street from the museum where Piero della Francesca's major painting lives—a good inspiration. Bruno, another resourceful antiques dealer from down the hill in Camucia, helps me find carved bits to incorporate into bookcases. Sketch a design or show him a picture and he gathers enough old wood to have it made by his carpenter friend. Mention doors or frames or even statues of San

FRESCOES IN OUR FAVORITE BEDROOM AT HOTEL TORNABUONI BEACCI, FLORENCE

Francesco, and he combs the countryside. We've made four of these painted bookcases. The first of the three beds we've made is my favorite, though it looks as if it came from a Neapolitan bordello. I traced a headboard shape on newspaper. Bruno had it cut out of old wood, and we trucked it over to Umbertide to a restoration workshop. With two women artists, I worked out an ethereal design of two putti raising the sun with ribbons, assorted clouds, bands of gold, all on a scumbled blue background. It looked better on paper. Even so, waking up in that bed feels good because beds should be as fanciful and romantic as possible.

The movie of my book *Under the Tuscan Sun* carried the tag line: "Life offers you a thousand chances. All you have to do is take one." I found this a little unsettling. Would that it were true. But I do know that one's own imagination offers a thousand chances, and what you need to do is act on what your instinct tells you. I took a risk buying a house in a foreign country. Another when I quit my teaching job to become a full-time writer. *Will I ever write another book?* Both decisions opened my future to a larger space. Via my books, my long passion for houses now has led me into partnership with manufacturers of furniture, linens, tableware, garden furniture, and lamps. I have had so much pleasure from these projects. The slow afternoons in the country houses and the early morning trips to antique markets and the weekend explorations of backstreets in Florence, all undertaken for the delight of knowledge, have created a new energy field and a network of exciting new friends. I imagine that the old signore would be amazed that the handed-down convent table, the lacemaker's chest, the beekeeper's bed, all the furniture they polished and cherished, would someday, like their cousins and uncles, migrate to America.

The house—the oldest game, a neglected philosophical and psychological subject, a location for everyday or sublime creativity, and a buffer between you and the wolf. The foundation touches earth and whatever spirits abide there rise through the walls and into your life.

LUCANI'S OLIVE OIL
HARVEST AT THE TOP OF
BRAMASOLE'S STAIRS

BACK GARDEN, PANTE'S VILLA CAPPUCCINI

Il Giardino Sotto il Sole

THE GARDEN UNDER THE SUN

Every garden should have a secret spot—a clematis arbor behind a curve of hedge, a big flat rock near a spring that flows in April, or a swing in the oldest tree. The secret resting place would be ideal with a bed, a wide chaise longue, or even a plot of long grass or moss. To fall asleep outside, day or night, bonds you quickly with the earth and gives a sense of *benessere*, well-being. A garden, taking a cue from the Viridarium, the Roman (and later Renaissance) pleasure gardens, is best when it imparts such private delights.

At Bramasole, the first secret spot that draws me outside is a stump-and-board bench on a high terrace overlooking the lake and valley. Before I sit down, I must bang the board against a tree to knock off all the ants. Then I'm happy. With a stunted oak tree for shelter and a never-ending view, I am hidden. No one knows where I am. The nine-year-old's thrill of the hideout under the hydrangea comes back: My mother is calling me and I am not answering.

BREAKFAST
IN THE HERB GARDEN
AT BRAMASOLE

My other secret place is a late-nineteenth-century iron gazebo just beyond my herb garden. A fig tree nearby lends its fructuous scent to that of roses, sage, rosemary, and rue. The fanciful Liberty (term in Italy for Art Nouveau) gazebo is a place to read, inside a bower of scented geraniums and lemon balm, imagining a century ago, when the signora who lived here relaxed by embroidering initials on handkerchiefs, after a spell of canning peaches in the afternoon sun.

I get too busy in Cortona, just as I do in California. In those times, I find that the *idea* of secret places in the garden is soothing. Garden rooms as places to entertain friends, places for an intimate chat, places for solitude, extend the idea of *la casa aperta*. These spiritual spots give pleasure to the *mind,* even when unused. Weeding the vegetable garden, working at my desk, running out to the umpteenth feast, packing to leave, I can glimpse the cupola of the gazebo or the high-up oak tree. I can go there in my imagination when I cannot find a solitary hour to visit with my yellow journal in the shade.

At Bramasole, I've always had an herb garden on the low terrace near the house where I can dash out with a basket and find what I need to light a spark in my roasting pan. Every year, however, when I returned for the summer, I found the herb garden overgrown, almost invisible. Beppe, who lovingly tends each olive, considers herbs and flowers strictly women's work. Although I found someone else to rescue my roses and beds in front of the house in my absence, the herb garden was always neglected. The tarragon bolted. The parsley became a lovely bush. The thyme died in the middle. Weeds led the rebellion. Cut hands, scratched arms, ripped pants, and a sense of déjà vu ensued, until I forced it back in shape again. Still, the impression remained scruffy.

The stones I lugged there for borders slipped haphazardly. My attempt to terrace with wooden beams looked sad.

Last summer I found Fabio. He came to cut down a leaning tree and stayed to whip our flower garden into the best shape it's ever seen. He knows when to prune. He *likes* flowers. I began to plan the herb garden as a place to stroll. I went to Barney's in Pistoia, where they have all the old varieties of roses, and came home with a car full of new colors and scents to plant among the herbs. Piero and Armando, master stonemasons, first repaired the stone wall all along the back of the terrace, and Fabio and his assistant, Bruno, built a bed along it, edging it with a low stone wall. I laid out a branching path around an elongated little island and Fabio lined the sides with bricks. At a building supply company out in the valley, I finally found the peach and white river pebbles I wanted for the path. Around here, gray stone is used for paths. Only gray. Literally every Tuscan who came by admired the garden but could not resist commenting on the (wrong) color of the stones. I found a few nineteenth-century iron chairs and had them painted a soft cream.

I love the undulating, mutating colors in this garden. Balls of santolina (cotton lavender) mixed with rosemary and a few types of lavender cover the terrace edge. In the island, rue offers a gentle silvery foliage, very soft, that with sage, borage, and variegated thymes looks especially fine under the garden's olive tree. I brought three new varieties of basil from France to go with the two local types I always plant. Hyssop and salvias grow fantastically well and offer lavender-blue flowers as well. All these happily took root in my herb garden in California, too.

Of the new roses, I prefer the Rita Levi-Montalcini, an apricot beauty named for an Italian woman who won the Nobel Prize in science. Since great accomplishments by women always make me feel stronger, I especially like this delicate rose, whose light fragrance blends synesthetically with the neighboring mints. The old-fashioned beauty, Reine des Violettes, on the other side of the mint, fascinates with its petals ranging

BRAMASOLE

A PLACE FOR
DREAMING AT
VILLA CETINALE

from baby pink to deep mauve. The blossoms look like the roses we made from Kleenex in kindergarten. This rose requires that you put your whole nose inside in order to inhale the grapy scent. Another I brought home, Gloire de Dijon, is also the title of a lovely poem by D. H. Lawrence, in which he compares a woman bathing to this rose. Her silver shoulders are like "wet and falling roses," and when she stoops to bathe, "her swung breasts / Sway like full-blown yellow / Gloire de Dijon roses." The poem ends:

> In the window full of sunlight
> Concentrates her golden shadow
> Fold on fold, until it glows as
> Mellow as the glory roses.

All those lovely *o* sounds in the last two lines seem right as I cup one of the blossoms in my hand. When I read the poem I always think of Bonnard's bathers; now I have the scent of the rose to add to the nuanced colors of the poem. The luminous, yellow fluffy blooms lend their vanilla and orange fragrance to their neighbor, the garlicky chives, especially after rain. I planted a new Paul Neyron, one of my favorites for its pure rose scent. My original one shrank a little every year until only a twig sent out one poor flower. I have around fifty different kinds of roses at Bramasole. Our friend Lucio comes by in late February and prunes them mercilessly, almost back to the ground. By April they're sending out vigorous shoots and in June the fun begins. Even into December, the roses are giving their last gifts.

In the herb garden, I found my special spot for breakfast—a small table beside a bank of rustic rugosas that bloom all summer. Because we love the inside/outside life, we have several places to eat in the garden. We set a little round lunch table on an upstairs terrace when we are sunning and reading on the chaise longues after a morning of work. We serve summer dinners at a tile-topped dining table under the lindens. Our main outside dining takes place just outside the kitchen at a square iron

table that once belonged to the writer Alberto Moravia. We have other places to live too. Out at the end of our land, we leave two sling chairs where we sink for a late afternoon glass of wine overlooking the distant lake and a sinuous line of cypresses. Ed takes the blue; I take the yellow. Who knows why these little habits form? In the Rose Walk garden, we have two chairs and a low table, a perfect spot for looking up at the stars and watching moonlight travel across the valley.

The herb garden evokes the early Italian gardens of simples, where medicinal and culinary plants for the household or the monastery were cultivated. Monks raised plants for their curative elixirs. Some were cultivated to repel moths, scent soaps, dye clothes, flavor liqueurs, and to season and add color to what was simmering in the fireplace. Others had uses lost to us now. Pennyroyal tea was thought to cause abortion. Santolina branches were laid on church floors to cut body odor.

I used to wonder why potted lemons are such a focus in the gardens of Tuscany, where the climate turns harsh enough in winter that they must be moved inside. Pots require a *limonaia,* a glass-fronted lemon house where they can receive the pale sun and bide their time until they are hoisted outside in April. I have torn a ligament in my back in this twice-yearly labor. Though we have a cart especially made for this task, the pots still must be maneuvered onto the platform. For six weeks I barely could walk. Turning over in bed was agony. I sat up like a horror-movie mummy rising from the dead. With all those monumental lemons, why is lemon not extensively used in local cooking? I read the early cookbooks—not a drop of juice or a strip of peel. Finally I learned that the lemon originally was cultivated for medicinal purposes. Apparently, the Tuscans knew that lemons promoted health long before the causes of scurvy were discovered. We have two dozen of these portable trees in Italy. In California, we can plant them in the ground. Now we wouldn't consider a garden without them. They carry, along with whiffs of their romantic perfume, the essence of the Tuscan garden.

At the first moment the medieval era's warring, siege mentality could be relaxed a bit, the concept of "simple" enlarged to include walled, secret gardens, where the women of the house would be free to stroll in privacy among the topiary. Although the gardens maintained the earlier purposes of the simple gardens, flower beds and fruit trees were planted. Boxwood bowers and wood or brick pergolas were added. All these became fixtures of the future Italian gardens. As the Renaissance dawned, the elaborate architectural extravaganzas of the first pleasure gardens became a necessary part of every villa.

Still sprouting in the collective memory of Italians are the gardens of the early Romans, especially Pliny's gardens in his country retreat in Tuscany and the gardens at Pompeii and Herculaneum. In the paintings at Herculaneum, we see the homey detail of window boxes spilling with flowers. Since Pompeii was originally a Greek settlement, the more than five hundred archeological remains of gardens sometimes echo that influence. You entered the Pompeiian house through the peristyle, that most felicitous structure. This courtyard had a fountain in the center so the musical fall of water greeted you. Paved with mosaic or patterned pebbles, the courtyard sloped slightly to a drain that took rainwater to a cistern below. The peristyle was surrounded by the painted walls of the house. Depicting gardens, these decorative paintings made the courtyard garden seem larger. This design still seems to me the happiest of arrangements for turning your key in the lock and coming home. Adjacent to the house, you often find a separate, walled garden—the predecessor of the garden of simples. At Pompeii, they grew herbs there and also the household's plants for wreaths and garlands, perfumes, and offerings to various gods. On one trip, Ed read long sections of Wilhelmina Jashemski's book about the gardens of Pompeii aloud to me in bed at night. A good companion volume is *Gardens of Pompeii*, written more recently, by Annamaria Ciarallo. The writings of Pliny (62–114) amaze because so many of the literal roots of Italian gardens were in full use in his Tuscan garden in Tusci, which no one has yet located. I am especially intrigued by how much he valued the element of surprise in a garden. Here's a description he wrote:

> *Many paths are separated by box [boxwood]. In one place you have a little meadow. In another place the box is set in groups, and cut into a thousand different forms. Sometimes the letters express the name of the owner, or that of the designer. Here and there little obelisks rise, mixed alternately with apple trees. . . . Then come a variety of figures and names cut in box.*
>
> *At the upper end of the garden is a semicircular bench of white marble. It is shaded with a vine which is trained upon four small columns of Carystian marble. Water gushes from several pipes under this bench, as if it were pressed out by the weight of the persons who sit upon it. The water falls into a stone cistern underneath, from whence it is received into a fine polished marble basin, so artfully contrived that it is always full without ever overflowing. When I eat here, the tray of dishes is placed around the margin, while the smaller dishes swim about in the form of little ships and waterfowl. Opposite this is a fountain which is incessantly emptying and filling, for the water which it throws up to a great height falling back again into it, is by means of connected openings returned as fast as it is received. . . .*
>
> *In different quarters are disposed several marble seats, which serve as so many reliefs after one is wearied of walking. Next to each seat is a little fountain.*

Signor Pliny, what do you make of the hot tubs and outdoor kitchens that are so popular in American gardens? I think you would drop your toga in *un momento romano* and jump in, after indulging in a big pulled-pork barbecue.

The writings of Tacitus, Varro, and Pliny and our visits to Pompeii propelled me into a study and tour of Italian gardens that I hope never ends.

⊷⊶

The Medici villas' gardens are a short excursion from Florence. Walking in them, I have the same strange lost feeling I have in the California Gold Country ghost towns. Their dramas, romance, and history are long past. The gardens remain as a palimpsest of former glory. Built to impress upon any visitor the power of the owners, the gardens still perform that function—and still are worth the trip, even in the rain and wind. I bring my hooded jacket and umbrella and take a taxi from the hotel where we are spending a couple of days. We adore Florence in the fall and winter when it becomes a city unto itself after the tourist onslaught. Ed wants to walk around town. He needs new boots. We agree to meet later for lunch at a wine bar. He has seen a couple of the Medici villas and finds that more than enough.

I enter the grounds of the Villa Petraia through a passageway between tall hedges. At the end I turn and see the grand old heap of a house, standing lonely and austere above its garden. The cropped watchtower recalls a time when the Pisans laid siege and were defeated. Not really beautiful, the vast building nevertheless radiates solidity and the enticement of a place with a long hold on the imagination. In the late 1800s, relatively recent history, Rosina, morganatic second wife of King Vittorio Emmanuele, fell in love with Villa Petraia, which had been stripped of its treasures. She went into decorating frenzy and moved antique furniture, tapestries, and paintings from many state-owned villas into Petraia, reviving the life of the house.

I hold my hood strings under my chin; the wind is turning over some of the citrus pots. Old boxwood borders surround empty flower beds. Where the Medicis had their neat quincunx orchards, the ground is fallow and forsaken. Oddly, there are dozens of absurdly small pots of plumbago lining the steps, all blown over. Someone must have to water them constantly.

Once a country paradise, this villa now languishes. From the stone terrace along the front, I can imagine the dreamy view down onto the formal beds with the dwarf peach trees all in bloom and the broad vista of countryside in the distance. In the misty rain, the outlook is melancholy. On the side of the villa, a ruined treehouse, built by those nineteenth-century Savoy royals, reminds me that actual people once lived here.

VILLA LA GAMBERAIA

Maybe the forlorn aspect of the historic gardens can jolt the senses in a way that a clipped and perfect garden could not. Or so I tell myself, as I walk downhill in the gusty rain.

Down the road from Petraia, I stop at a baroque villa right on the road, Villa Corsini. The *portone* is open. I step into the empty courtyard and look into the caretaker's niche, where a woman plays solitaire with a cat on her lap. She waves me toward one open room but does not bother to rise. What a wonder—the architecture dazzles. The stairs up to the villa's main rooms are cordoned. The courtyard has several fine, dust-covered Etruscan sarcophagi and some equally dirty marble statues that would be the pride of a collection in most of the world. I go back in a moment and ask the woman if she can turn on the lights in the dim room. The gloom disappears and I'm in an enchanting frescoed salon, the end of which is glassed. Below, a wondrous garden once bloomed but its paths are now deserted, the flowers spent. These forsaken gardens must come to life in summer when whatever is left there blooms. I muse a while in the room, imagining breakfast overlooking the rose garden, a chaise longue of blue silk, with the friendly pastoral frescoes to keep everyone company. The salon, of course, is furnished only with my fantasies. I cross the courtyard to ask the woman with the cat. "Signora, who is the painter of the frescoes?"

"Niccolò Cantestabile," she replies without looking up. Or did she say *Con*testabile—not that I've heard of either. She slaps down the cards onto an upturned box. I return to the idyllic scenes. I'm reveling in the privacy of looking at the country scenes on the walls and the garden outside with no one else around. Someone had marvelous days in that room. *Grazie mille,* I call to the caretaker, but she is in her own world.

Down the road, Villa di Castello stands long and low with a capricious placement of windows. From any one of them, you would look out at expansive upward-sloping gardens. This is the reverse of most positioning, where you look down on flat or downward-sloping gardens. The slight incline invites you into its paths and geometric shapes. From a bedroom window in the house, the garden must, to a sleepy glance, look like Renaissance brocade or an intricate Oriental rug.

I am the only one crazy enough to be out on this windy day. My red umbrella has been jerked inside out twice and my hair must look like Medusa's. The emptiness lets me wonder. What life would come back to the place with a hundred children playing on the lawns, hiding among the majestic lemon pots, sailing boats in the fountains?

Cosimo de' Medici gave ambitious shape to the garden in 1538. Consciously, according to the chronicler Vasari, he enhanced the idea of his own greatness and royalty through the make-no-mistake splendor of this garden. The extensive water features—lake, aqueduct, grand fountains—were meant to reflect the Medici naval power. This is lost on the present-day viewer, but ontologically, that was the message with the garden as the medium. Serendipitously, it became a paradigm for all the Renaissance gardens, in Italy and the rest of the Continent.

I'm fascinated by the Medicis—the combination of artistic fervor and ruthless will. And I'm fascinated by the fact of this place in the here and now. To reimagine is not necessarily to lessen. Let's start a great cooking school in one end of the villa, with the students serving lunch to visitors and tending herb and vegetable gardens. Surely some lively way to both protect the patrimony and keep the atmosphere of the tomb away is possible for these buildings. Turn on the water in all the happy fountains! But obviously the government cannot keep all Italy's vast inheritances in top condition. Italy has schools, hospitals, and highways to support and endless social needs to fill. And Italy has exponentially more art to protect than any country in the world. Would someone please, at least, organize fifty garden clubs in Florence? Each one could maintain one section of a historic garden. Citizens, escape the tourists huffing in the July heat, go work on the land, take a picnic, trim the roses.

This garden is much more tended than Petraia. Five hundred magnificent potted lemons line the levels of the garden. Some are enormous. The scent of lemon blossoms layers with the heavier perfume of Indian jasmine, *mugherino,* cultivated here since 1688, when the King of Portugal gave plants to the grand duke. A special winter house for the jasmine is called the *stufa dei mugherini,* the jasmines' stove. I am happy that I don't have to help move these lemons into the *limonaia* for the cold months. Broad paths and noble busts invite me to stroll, but the rain is turning icy and I search my bag for my phone, hoping I have enough charge left to call a taxi.

Three minutes, they promise. I wait under a tree for fifteen, writing in my notebook. What did I learn for my own gardens from visiting these gardens in the rain?

❀ Jasmine pots next to the lemons. The two scents complement each other quite divinely.

❀ Bigger pots for lemons, alternating with smaller pots.

❀ A line of pots can delineate a wall of a garden "room." The pots look especially architectural when placed laterally up a hillside. This is one of the elements that gives Castello a rhythmic feeling.

❀ Dwarf fruit trees, so widely planted in boxwood beds in the sixteenth century, still anchor a small bed, giving some height without dominance.

❀ The folly of small pots in a big garden.

❀ Boxwood is immortal.

I've exported so many other ideas from Tuscan gardens to my California garden:

❀ Plump olive oil jars planted with trailing geraniums and placed for emphasis amid various flower beds.

❀ Terra-cotta urns planted simply with asparagus fern, boxwood balls, or rosemary cut into obelisks. I rotate these from front porch to terrace to the circle of pebbles around the fountain.

❀ More "furniture"—rustic stone benches, rusty chairs sprayed Greek blue, tall iron crosses and willow tepees for climbing plants, stone balls, marble-topped tables.

❀ A terrace wall or fence lined with big pots of white hydrangeas. A path up to the next level in the garden lined with pots of pink hydrangeas.

- Groups of cypress trees, different heights, planted on an eminence, or around water for their reflections and spatial relations.
- Olive trees scattered in the garden. They lend a timeless quality. Well-pruned, they hardly shade the plants below but offer their shimmering leaves to the rhythm of the garden and offer exclamation points and height to delight the eye.
- A row of iron arches. What could be simpler? Planted with mixed clematis, morning glory, and climbing roses, all of which twine, mingle, and span a long season of bloom.

The taxi driver offers his opinion that the rich knew how to live in the old days. I agree.

Ed is waiting outside Caffè Italia under his huge green shepherd's umbrella. The sight of it makes me want to go back right now to the fresh autumn hills of Cortona.

My favorite gardens are the ones still inhabited by someone whose love can be felt in the ongoing work. Passion escapes imposed rigor and inhabits a realm where you feel, as philosopher Merleau-Ponty said, "the spontaneous surge of the life-world." The gardens I love, rather than study, occupy smaller space. Perhaps the large formal gardens feel theoretical, too remote.

La Foce was the garden of Iris Origo, one of my heroes. Her book *War in the Val d'Orcia* chronicles her marriage to Antonio Origo, an Italian marchese, and their monumental restoration of a house, two thousand acres, and many farm buildings, starting in 1924. Daunting stories of bringing water through a pipe seven miles long make our well-drilling episodes seem tame. In World War II, when the retreating Germans neared their home, the Origos marched across the countryside with the group of children they were sheltering from war-torn Italian cities. The story is deeply moving. Her autobiographical *War in the Val d'Orcia* and *Images and Shadows* have the power to re-create her personal world. To the reader, it can seem odd that you feel close to the writer of books you love and she does not know you at all. She's on my list of people long dead whom I would have liked to have met.

Along with the rebuilding of stone tenant houses, Iris Origo created a poetic garden, which is nurtured today by her daughter, Benedetta. The Englishman Cecil Pinsent was instrumental in the design, as he was at I Tatti, home of Bernard Berenson, now a part of Harvard University.

Since Benedetta is a friend of our friend Alain, she invites us for lunch. Afterward, she shows us her mother's study, a book-lined room with comfortable places to sit. I feel another twinge of regret. I would like to be handed a flowered cup of tea and to hear from Iris about her new writing project. Isn't it a little eerie to walk through an extremely personal house when the creator of it is gone forever? The *house* is still living. The waxy gleam of the terra-cotta floors suddenly seems like water to me and I become momentarily dizzy.

Benedetta takes us on a personal tour of the garden. We imagine the wisteria pergola is in bloom, dripping clusters swarming with bees. Lawns are interrupted by box beds, from the middle of which spring plain old lavender—lovely. La Foce feels intimate. What a joy to escape the drive of the pen and wander, as the writer must have, until a surge of inspiration drove her back to that book-lined room. The garden is, as the Italians would perceive it, new. Although started in 1927, it seems older, quite settled into the landscape. This is an illusion, for this garden actually is a green oasis in the sere and dramatic Sienese countryside. Vines clambering up the walls, a table for dining under a rose arbor, and swings for children all give a sense of ease within a very personal garden.

The hills above Florence must be one of the most idyllic places to live on this earth. Gentle olive groves, the views of the Arno Valley and the monadnock-dome of the duomo, and the blissful climate—this would suffice. The plus, naturally, is Florence itself. The number-ten bus takes you to Settignano in fifteen minutes. On the way, Ed and I pass dozens of places that make me think, *I could live here.* The Villa Gamberaia is the most idyllic of the idyllic villas. Usually I don't enjoy going inside stately homes where a docent talks endlessly about the restoration of the bedcovers, but I would love to see every inch of La Gamberaia. Too bad the house is not open to the hoi polloi. What gives this house such dignity? The uncompromising square situated on a broad platform of land, the mellow gold walls and the rigorous symmetry of the façade. No one in its four-hundred-year history ever has added an unfortunate kitchen wing or dinky conservatory. The brochure drawing shows an interior courtyard. I'm already in love. The villa, solid and proud, has large windows, all curtained now. Easy to imagine someone running through the house yanking each pair of draperies open to the ample summer sun. Easy to imagine a small boy practicing the violin, his mother at her easel. Such a house engenders creativity.

The gardens, extending in all directions around the house, are humanly scaled and friendly. Nothing is planted close to the house, which adds to the sense that it simply rose out of the ground, an inevitable archetype. No shrub, no rose. Ah, the sublime austerity.

The name of the house translates as "the shrimpery." Centuries ago the household kept a pond where crayfish (*gamberi*) were raised. At another place in the garden there was once a rabbit island. Bunnies heading eventually for the roasting pan doubling as garden ornaments—something to ponder.

Because of their architectural nature, Italian gardens are rewarding to visit in all seasons. Since design elements predominate, flowers are not crucial, as they are in English gardens. But at La Gamberaia in winter, we both longed to see the garden in June with the peonies, hydrangeas, and roses blooming in the romantic upper terrace. That section of the garden is all balustrades, busts, shell-and-pebble walls, and stairs leading up to the lemon garden and down into the densely planted *selvatico*, wood. There are two of these small woods. I think they must have once been *ragnaie*, copses, where birds were lured by blinded thrushes tied to the shrubs or set out in cages. Nets were thrown over for very easy hunting. Within the overgrown *ragnaia* remnants, Hansel and Gretel could materialize, dropping crumbs.

A formal *broderie* (embroidery) is usually the star of a villa garden—the intricate box-edged beds in a highly geometric design. Villa Gamberaia also has such a garden on its south side but here, instead of roses, dwarf fruit trees, or other flowers inside the beds, you find pools. The water aspect was added early in the twentieth century. Water doubles the garden with its reflections of roses, hedges, and an enormous box ball, and gives the prospect an ethereal air unlike any other garden I know.

I'm intrigued by the elusive aspect of gardens. No written description can capture the spirit of a garden. A photograph or painting of a garden is bound to be a detail of the whole. Even in memory, the greens blend and the views shift. If you want to capture the essence of a garden, for memory's sake, you look for emblems. Someone whimsically painted La Gamberaia's chapel wall with two trompe l'oeil windows. The olive grove begins just below the house, reminding me that these historic villas always were close to their agricultural roots. The only ornament in front of the villa is a modest well, even now climbing with creamy yellow Crépuscule roses. A homey detail, but symbolic of the live-here ambiance of this garden. I will remember these little visions.

If a fairy godmother flew in my study window this morning and said, "You can choose among all the villas and gardens. You can have any one you want," I would hesitate only a moment before saying, "Villa Cetinale."

Steven, with his cameras, and I set off early one October morning from Bramasole. He is in the process of designing his garden in St. Helena, California, another slice of paradise on this planet. I am thinking of the broad low terrace at Bramasole, an olive grove and former potato patch, waiting for inspiration. We are ready to be overwhelmed. And we are.

Villa Cetinale is situated behind a complex of old annexes and farm buildings, which keeps it firmly placed in the landscape where grapes and olives and wheat, that ancient triumvirate, have been grown forever. Beyond the ugly gate, you truly enter a world defined by the garden. "Not in Kansas," I say as we enter. We see an ancient man in slippers leaving the house. With flyaway white hair and rough wool plaid shirt and country pants, he could be a family retainer or someone about to turn into a prince, but, instead, we meet Lord Lambton, the English owner who restored the garden. He stops to chat for a while and then waves us into his kingdom.

The villa has no touch of the fortress mentality. The design seems feminine, with a three-arched loggia connecting to humanly scaled wings. The second story repeats the loggia motif, with the baffled arches framing windows and balustrades. As we walk closer, we see the coats of arms of the ancient Chigi banking family, who began work here in 1676. The villa seems to glow—the warm yellow-gold feels as though it pulsates light. This is the most mysterious of gardens, and at the same time, the friendliest. And, ah!—the paths are not gray stone but the warm pinkish cream ones I was reprimanded for selecting at Bramasole. The gardens around the house beckon the dreamer—long pergolas that are tunnels of green, a sweet family chapel, and a clock tower that looks borrowed from *Alice's Adventures in Wonderland*. An empty swimming pool, once glamorous, conjures visions of the younger Lord Lambton's friends sipping gin fizzes back when the sun had not set on the Empire and the English gentry fell in love with Tuscany. They would have known the sonnets of Elizabeth Barrett Browning. All the tidy clipped boxwoods bask in the warm October sun. I wonder if perhaps these embroidered parterres link, somewhere way back, with the labyrinths once laid out to simulate a circuitous pilgrimage to the Holy Land.

Steven and I notice the same things for our own gardens:

※ Line a walk or drive on either side with big potted lemons (or clipped rosemary or box) for instant architectural interest and strong definition.

※ Place big pots on ten-inch squares of stone—more architecture, as well as more stability.

※ First define a shaped space around the house, then plan the rest of the garden out from there. At Cetinale, the shape around the house is a rounded square, bordered

VILLA CETINALE, NEAR SIENNA

with boxwood and lemons. The house then floats on this defined extension of its perimeter.

※ Pergolas on either side of a rectangular garden add mystery and provide at the end a place to link the two with a swath of grass and borders of flowers.

※ Boxwood balls—requiring little care—anchor beds, punctuate spaces, stay green in winter, and work with either spilling, flowering plants or with more formal rose and peony bushes.

Beyond the house's immediate gardens, the mystery of Cetinale deepens. The wooded areas, a traditional part of all villa gardens, here are called the Thebaide. This name comes from the third-century desert fathers near the ancient Egyptian city of Thebes, who escaped to wilderness in order to pursue hermetic lives as atonement for sins. One of the Chigis devised this wood as a place where he could pray for forgiveness for having killed a rival and living a rambunctious life. What remains are votive chapels, a canopy of trees, and the flash of a red fox. Steven and I, both in our private meanderings, meet here and there and say at once, "Don't you *love* this?"

More enchanting still, at the end of a long cypress avenue, the land abruptly rises. Over two hundred steep steps lead to a *romitorio*, a five-story dwelling for hermits, built in 1713. Closed now for restoration, this marvel, the end of the long axis of the garden, causes the visitor to stop and absorb the astounding surprise. Hermits once looked down on the garden and beyond into the Sienese hills. Imaginatively, we look down too on the magnificent folly that is a garden. Nature always waits to reclaim such spaces—and there's the charm, the tension. For a while, you carve out your desires on the face of the earth. *Per ora . . .* In a garden such as this, the result can be enduring.

En route home, we stop at a roadside trattoria in Castelnuovo Berardenga, one of those fortuitous by-chance encounters with the truly local people and food. We order pasta with *funghi porcini* and a little *quarto* of the wine from the grapes right outside the window. Everyone orders a plate of fried artichokes so we do too, as we try to sort out the genius of Italian gardens. We find that two things are essential:

※ A careful garden design with the house as the center, and the garden "rooms" just as delineated as the rooms within the house. These outdoor rooms have different functions, just as the interior spaces have. Theater performances, lawn games such as bocce, meditative strolls, hunting areas, places for the raising of fish and rabbits, retreats from the heat—all these uses of the garden caused separate areas to be designed and elaborated upon. Someone thought of alternating sunlight and shadow, coolness and warmth. That all villa gardens have a wood seems symbolic to me. You enter a Dantean wood and you exit into light.

※ Simplified elements endlessly amplified. I tell Steven about my first edition of *Italian Villas and Their Gardens* by Edith Wharton, with illustrations by Maxfield Parrish. She's a good companion on my garden trips. She wrote that the Italian garden's permanent effects are independent of seasons because they are made of "marble, water, perennial verdure." I'd add stone to that list. She's right—trimmed box, ilex, hornbeam, along with cypress trees adding their lengthy presence and shadow, sculpt the garden. Espaliered fruit along the walls add a bas-relief to the green sculptures of balls, cones, obelisks, hedges, tunnels—the endless variety and play of shapes were part of the design from the first.

Salute, Lord Lambton. We'll return to see the wall of wisteria in bloom.

⌖

Sunday, an afternoon for a walk after a long *pranzo* of Placido's roasted guinea hen and wild pigeon. "Are you *sure* you didn't trap these in the piazza?" we tease. The men, one of whom has the angelic name Serafino, play cards. Someone sleeps on a bench in the sun. Some of us look at Chiara's photos from when she visited us in California.

AFTER PRANZO

The October days grow short. Even at four, our road is striped with cypress shadows. The sun hovers at the top of the hill, about to disappear behind the jagged stone wall of the Medici fortress. The serene conical trees turn blue-green as the sky deepens toward twilight. Below us spread the just-picked olive orchards, shimmering pewter, silver, mercury in the transparent last sunlight. All of Tuscany resembles a garden. Ed and I walk up to Torreone, curve back up the Santa Margherita road, and pass our upper neighbor, out walking his mother-in-law, hunched and gone into the realms of Alzheimer's. He walks slowly. Patiently. She hangs on his arm. She stares at the ground. He looks out at the valley and beyond to the hills. *From whence cometh my help.* We, too, look at these hills glazed with warped golden rays angling across the Val di Chiana plain. A god could surf in on those rays. We talk about our latest project, rebuilding the deep cistern at the bottom of our terraces. No choice—it collapsed. After all the gardens I've seen, I want to haul in a lot more boxwood. Ed wants to reduce the number of annual plantings we do every year and establish a more enduring garden. "No more of those sprawling yellow petunias. No more dahlias to mildew." We want to naturalize daffodils, orange lilies, and irises again where some of our wall-building has destroyed them.

"How many bulbs will it take?" I wonder.

"I'd say five thousand," Ed guesses.

"Dig five thousand holes. Put in a scoop of bonemeal—that makes my back hurt just to hear the words. Let's just let that wild potato vine take the hillsides."

"Would your Lord Lambton approve?"

I want to visit all the gardens in my guidebook. It's fun to view gardens practically, but even if no specific idea results, there is something fundamentally affirmative about connecting with the mind and hands that create the magic borderland between house and world. The meditative zone. The arena for play. The prayer bower. The friends' room. The corner for beauty. The connective tissue of pure sensation. The strange *romitorio* will live in my mind. So will the rabbit island, the water parterre, my own gazebo, the dense copses where birds were snared. And the fountains and statues that you suddenly come upon as you round a curve or reach the end of a cypress allée—magical presences to evoke the idea that all of life is a drama waiting to be enacted.

Another neighbor is out walking her dog. She's plump and bundled into a red plaid jacket. She greets us. "I had a dream about you," she says. Her little dog yaps and snaps at my heels. "Not about you but about your beautiful garden. I dreamed the Madonna and Mother Teresa were conversing in Bramasole's garden. The roses were all in bloom. I'm sure the two of them were there for a reason."

I'm enchanted. As we walk away, I have a full vision of the two holy women whispering together in the midst of all the sunny yellow blooms. I say to Ed, "Isn't that an amazing dream? Miraculous?"

He laughs. "Yes, and all it lacks is Donatella Versace doing the laundry." This surreal addition forms an unholy trinity. Surprise is the best gift of all in the garden.

RAGS
CENCI

These "rags" are traditionally made in Tuscany during *Carnevale* (literally, "farewell to meat"), the time right before Lent begins. Eat them while they're still warm—you won't be able to stop at just one *cencio*. In Cortona, you'll hear them called *stracci* and *frappe*, other Tuscan words for rags.

3 TABLESPOONS SUGAR
3 TABLESPOONS BUTTER
2 CUPS FLOUR
3 EGG YOLKS
PINCH OF SALT
7 TABLESPOONS GRAPPA OR BRANDY
1 CUP PEANUT OIL
CONFECTIONERS' SUGAR, AS NEEDED

Blend the sugar and butter, then work this into the flour. Make a well for the yolks. Mix salt and grappa and add to the well. Knead together to make a firm dough. Let rest for 10 minutes. Roll out on a floured surface until quite thin. Cut in strips about 2 inches wide and 8 inches long. Make a vertical slit near the top of each, then pull the bottom of the strip through, forming a loop with a tail. Fry in batches in hot oil for about 4 minutes and drain on paper towels. When cool, sift confectioners' sugar on top.

MAKES ABOUT 21/2 DOZEN *CENCI*

BORGO DI VAGLI, CORTONA

STONES FOR THE FONT OF LEAVES HOUSE

Although we do not drive a four-wheel-drive vehicle, our car has become adept on roads it never was meant to negotiate. Briars slash the metallic blue paint, and a layer of mud rims the fenders. My red rubber boots live in the trunk. We have developed a passion for abandoned *borghi,* tiny villages, church ruins, and scattered farms far in the Tuscan mountains.

The villages, mostly empty since World War II, were built hundreds of years ago for farmers, woodcutters, and shepherds, usually for twenty to thirty families. With miles of mountains around, you'd expect the houses to scatter up and down the hills, but no. The stone houses cluster together as tight as a fist. I am sure the historian would say there's safety in numbers and that medieval mercenaries regularly marauded the countryside. Certainly that's true, but I'm guessing there's another reason, too—the genetic conviviality of the Italians and the preference for togetherness. This preference astonishes my North American instinct for privacy. On the autostrada, traffic jams provide an excuse to get

AURORA AND FULVIO

out of the car and chat. If I am the only person sitting on a bus and someone boards, I'm stunned and thrilled when she lumbers up the aisle and sits down beside me. Unexpected, but somehow right. Why not attach your house to the Zappini's, and isn't it fortunate that the Agnolucci family lives to the left under the fig trees? If I am cooking pheasant, my neighbor catches the scent. If she is mad at her father-in-law, I'll be the second to hear. Everyone works for the local marchese, but he's far away in his castello drinking mead and feeling feudal. Ed offers the necessary corrective. "Big families were packed cheek by jowl into these small rooms."

Architecturally, the result is a pleasing cohesiveness to the eye; each house unites or relates to the others, just as intensely as the inhabitants must have.

Scrambling around one of these places relinquished to time, you sense those vanished lives. The most lost-in-time *borghi* have moss-edged stone roofs, embroidered with yellow and gray lichen. The beauty strikes you as organic. You can feel the rough hands that hauled the stones out of the fields and passed them up to a cousin, who overlapped them with such skill that no rain could seep inside the house. You can see the intelligence behind the choice of the site, with an orientation toward the most sun possible. Inevitably, a pure spring gushes from a hillside. Sometimes, we'll come upon the community bread oven, often collapsed. If there's a church, its rounded apse echoes the shape of the oven's domed interior. Why do the houses seem to rise naturally out of the land? Because they did—simply pick up nine thousand stones from the field or chip them from an outcropping, haul them back, and there's your natural house. Who planted the wisteria still climbing through a window? The drooping, ashen-purple clusters send out a rainy, wistful perfume.

The deserted *borghi* work powerfully on the imagination. We often revisit the hidden thirteenth-century church of San Donato with its attached rectory above a well-preserved empty *borgo.* The celestial paint still falls off in chunks, and the roof faltered and sank years ago. I lift an iron-ringed stone on the floor, and shafts of sunlight strike a huddle of bones in the crypt below. I drop the stone and run. A saint? A martyr? Or the village priest who used to toast his feet by the rectory fireplace, still filled with charred wood? We too once built a fire in a half-standing house when sleet stopped our mushroom hunting.

Many times we have searched for the church of San Michele, adding another stone scrape to the car, but we never have found it. We don't care. The pleasure is the quest, the afternoons when we never meet a car, impromptu picnics of wild strawberries and a sun-baked bottle of mineral water from the backseat, and walks through meadows of poppies.

We assumed these crumbling, secret haunts of ours were irreclaimable. Then we found Sogna. We'd gone with friends in search of a restaurant, Le Antiche Sere (The Antique Evenings) located in the *borgo.* Over the valley, down the Siena road, a right turn onto a white road, and then through pastoral countryside, we came to an amazing sight: the *borgo* Sogna, brought back from ruin. This idyllic village dozing in the sun, we learned, had seized the imagination of Fulvio Di Rosa several years ago and he determined to save it. We were especially captivated by his placement of modern sculptures among the old stones. I wanted to meet him, and shortly did, through a friend of a friend.

He stood in the doorway of Le Antiche Sere, very tanned, very fit. *A man who knows who he is,* I thought immediately. Later, I would get to know his quixotic humor, his flashes of anger at any slowness or incompetence, and, most of all, his brilliance.

He walks me through the village. He has a passion for his heritage and knows how to rebuild structures while respecting their integrity. After eight years of working on contemporary projects in Brazil, he returned to Italy and began ambitious restorations. Sogna, he says, is actually his third *borgo.* He's a visionary, with energy like a brush fire. Since in my next life I will be an architect, I have paid a great deal of attention to buildings in this life, especially to the houses in the Tuscan vernacular. Fulvio does the most meticulous and artistic work I have seen.

Knowledge of the superior destroys you for the ordinary. Unfortunately, since seeing his work, I hate most restorations, where every nuance of craft has gone over to the powers of the cement mixer—cement totally erases the stonemason's art.

Sogna, instead, looks as if time rolled back, showing the village as it once was. No wires, no shiny brick, no kitsch, no artificial landscaping. Here's the dignity of simplicity.

We then have several dinners at Sogna. I tuck their handwritten menus into my yellow writing book. Fulvio and his wife, Aurora, sponsor concerts of avant-garde music in the chapel he restored. Each raucous and shocking concert is followed by a splendid dinner for twenty or so close friends. We begin to be invited, then we invite them to Bramasole. We talk nonstop about architecture and authenticity in design. We exchange great bottles of wine and recipes. Though they've lived for years in Tuscany, both Fulvio and Aurora are from Piemonte. We begin to know more about the wines of that area and their risottos made with Barolo or melon. Then we begin going with them to festas in the countryside, adventurous restaurants (fried wisteria? fried *sambuco* flowers?), and visiting artisans in the hills.

I am thrilled to have found such friends. *We laughed in the same places,* the poet Louise Bogan wrote. Laughter is a strong bond. I feel that I have an Italian brother. Aurora takes my arm as we walk, which makes me feel deliciously Italian.

Fulvio invites us to see his new project. This time he's taken on Vagli, a *borgo* in our neighborhood.

Leaving Cortona, driving toward Mercatale, you quickly enter a wilder Tuscany. We're often out this way to eat at Trattoria Mimmi in Mercatale, where you pass neat rows of lettuces and beans on the way to the door. En route, I'm always dazzled when, rounding a sudden curve, the *castello* La Rocca di Pierle rises before me. Even if you're not inclined toward the magical, this looming stone relic catapults you into thoughts of princesses and knights. Italy has many eleventh-century castles, but this is a paradigm. Quite simply, it looks immortal. A white road to the left winds around the *chiesetta,* little church, of San Biagio, and into the hills above Pierle. There lies Vagli. As we climb and dip, we're looking down onto the Rocca's crumbling three towers, where Sleeping Beauty, Rapunzel, and Briar Rose all must be hiding. There may be a more mystical view in Tuscany, but I don't know where.

Fulvio waves from the entrance of a muddy construction site. We see a classic *borgo* with exceptional stonework. Vagli is a residence club. I'd never really give up my house in Cortona, but I imagine not receiving midnight calls at home in California, seven thousand miles away, from someone asking what should be done about the broken pipe now shooting water into the stairwell. I would store a box of family photos, sauté pans, pillowcases, and books, unpack in a flash and begin my vacation. A nice twist of fate—from plowshare to timeshare.

ALL PHOTOS
BORGO DI VAGLI,
CORIONA

Given that the farmers probably will not be returning, I begin to plot new purposes for the hundreds of *borghi* in the Italian hills: music camps, artists' colonies, hospices, religious retreat centers. After all, easily taking the past into the future is part of the Italian genius for living.

As Ed and Fulvio linger over drainage pipes, I keep wandering off, wanting to see the rabbit hutch that will hide all the electrical connections, a curving stone staircase, the terraced levels for sunning and swimming. Everything from the toppled buildings has been saved for a new use: stone fireplaces refitted, broken beams reappearing as staircase supports, old planks forming cupboards and shelves, the original stone sinks simply left to be admired. I even see a salvaged pile of rusted handmade nails.

What I love are the stonework around the doors and windows, the steps worn to a slope in the middle, the ghosts of voices in the path-wide street, the rusted hand plows found in a pigpen and now set in the garden as sculpture. Most of all I love feeling the mysterious sense of lives in a remote and secret place. We point to lintels and portals farmers took from other buildings and put to use. When, in 1800, a window frame from 1400 collapses, why not hoist the one from the fallen plague hospital or the castle torched by mercenaries? At the top of one building, Fulvio shows us a sculpted, spooky human head and serpent in low relief—a little comic, a little sinister. I especially admire the unusual round windows, porthole-sized, beside many doors. I almost expect a ruddy face to look out.

The luscious yellow, salmon, and blue paints of the interior walls are mixed with earth then applied directly onto the plaster, creating a chalky, fresco color depth. The fourteenth-century grain growers certainly would be delighted with the seventeenth-century convent beds, new stone sinks, and hand-painted armoires.

Every detail contributes to a sense of *home*, a word that does not exist in Italian, but one that Fulvio understands well. He embodies the Jamesian dictum, "A painter can never be responsible *enough* for every inch of his canvas." He even designed the

sun-washed dishes and the cutlery. Hollowed into the wall, cupboards are closed by aged wooden doors called *stipi*. He combs the antique markets for these, and for the iron tables and chairs on his patios.

My hand is out—touching chestnut stair rails, brick treads, jigsaw-patterned stone floors, white marble counters, and especially the fabrics. Busatti in Anghiari still makes traditional Tuscan cotton and linen. I've used many patterns in my own house in Cortona. My mushroom-hunting socks come from there, too. The bright yellow dye derives from *ginestre,* broom flowers, in the spring months and from onions in winter. They reproduce the bright orange, brown, and red plaids the *contadini* used to tie up food they took to the fields. Some of their fabrics are copied from the Virgin Mary's dresses in paintings and from heraldic shields. At Vagli, Busatti's waffle-weave towels hang in the bathrooms and classic white woven spreads cover the beds as they have for generations. Busatti still makes rough gray wool undershirts that the farmers at Vagli surely wore and that one of the Busatti owners, Giovanni, showed me under his own shirt when I visited the factory. The Busatti family has been making linen and striped cotton and thick blankets ever since Napoleon passed this way. Naturally their fabrics look at home in the Tuscan landscape.

Dina, who lives below Vagli, in the village of Mercatale, waits for us at the end of our walk. With her grandmother's long rolling pin, she starts her work on a just-made disk of pasta. Soon she spins the dough like a frisbee. She flips and twirls the supple circle, rolls the pin all the way up to her elbows. I am watching a master. She removes her big board and sets the table with hand-painted pasta bowls. Fulvio opens the wine, as she sets down a loaf of bread and her meltingly light but toothsome homemade pasta with wild boar sauce. Then she brings a platter of her husband's *salumi,* including the traditional one made with fennel. I pretend that I will be climbing the stairs after dinner to the bedroom with the big iron bed, turning down the covers, looking out the round window at ten million stars, and in the distance, the dreaming towers of Pierle.

Vagli became my school. Ed, too, was captivated by the skill of the plasterer, Francesco, whose work made the walls seem alive, not squared-off and sprayed. Hidden in the first layer against the stone walls are millions of pinpoint-foam balls, which provide insulation in otherwise frigid stone rooms. The final plaster coats cover them. Each ground floor is taken up, excavated, and fitted with interlocking plastic igloos, which allow air to circulate and moisture to drain away. Then the old brick or stones are relaid by Sauro. Fulvio has found true practitioners of their crafts. Each careful segment of the work complements the others.

As we leave, we see men digging mud and rubble where last night a house wall collapsed onto a large tractor. When the tractor is unearthed, one of the workers hops on and turns the ignition. After one or two chugs, it starts. What paradise—a construction site.

On a late August day, a few months after our tour of Vagli, Ed and I are picking blackberries with our neighbor, Chiara. We follow a Roman road from Torreone up the slope of Monte Sant' Egidio. Chiara leads us to the sweetest blackberries on the mountain.

Just past a dry little riverbed, Ed points to a stone ruin. Soon we are scrambling through the brush. The house sits, broody and remote, beside a grove of old-growth chestnut trees. To the left, we see another heap, completely covered with vines. "Little Red Riding Hood, where are you? Come out," I call. We cannot get to the gaping doors because of the weeds, but we see adze-shaped small windows, which mark it as a very old structure, and the stone roof, parts of which have been replaced by cheap tile. A stone roof. One side of the house is collapsed.

Later, after the blackberry jam is sealed in jars, I ask our friend Rupert about the house. Because there are now so few country ruins left, he tends to know all of them. I'm shocked to hear him say, "Frances, the house is for sale and has been for several years. There's a bloody lot of work to do up there." He tells us that the last farmers to live there left shortly after World War II. "The count is in no hurry," he explains. "He's looking for the right person." This sounds oh-so-familiar to us since we'd heard versions of it when we were looking for a house in 1990.

The count lives in a secluded villa at the top of the mountain. He drives a venerable jeep, which we come to know well as we become friends. I have been bounced in the backs of many cars on Tuscan back roads, but never as profoundly as in the back of that relic. The properties that old Italian families can own staggers the imagination. If your ancestors have stayed in place since the eleventh century, they've had time to accumulate. He shows us everything—a monastery, shepherds' houses, a Roman bridge, an extensive fortress-like house with fascinating outbuildings, villas, and his own pine-enshrouded, romantic house with a fireplace big enough to sit inside. Fortunately, he's read my books and thinks we'll do right by the house. We are even more smitten when he tells us that the house was built by hermits who followed St. Francis of Assisi in the early thirteenth century. Down the hill and along the torrent into which "our" torrent flows, the great old beehive of a monastery, where St. Francis had a cell, still swarms with brown-robed monks. We often see them in our local bank with their long beards and bare feet. Their Sant' Egidio, for everyone in Cortona, is a sacred mountain.

The count shows us the oldest map he has. The spidery ink spells out a grand name for the rustic farm, Fonte delle Foglie, the source or font of leaves. He thinks the name comes from an Etruscan spring, where the house's water flowed. We troop through more weeds to find the tumbled stone springhouse, where just at the base a spring bubbles into a pool of water. Under the canopy of trees, the name suddenly makes sense. It poetically joins the greenery and water that most characterize the place.

Before we even sign the deeds, we think of Fulvio. In Tuscany, everyone has a secret *soprannome,* nickname. We have begun to call Fulvio "MegaMan" for the brand of vitamins he takes. We should invest in a few bottles ourselves, if his energy level can be duplicated. He could guide us through a historic restoration and we could witness the transformation. Already, we are determined to restore the ancient stone roof instead of replacing it with tile.

"Well, let's have a look," Fulvio agrees. We bounce *him* along the track leading to Fonte. When he gets out of the car, he merely says, "My goodness." Noncommittal, but I think I hear a note of wonder at the site—or maybe at the magnitude of the folly involved in restoration. Ed has cut a path to the house with the weed machine and a swath in the vine-covered heap near the house, enough to find a crumbled stone hay barn underneath. We step inside on the house's bottom floor, where the animals lived, sending their steamy heat up through the slightly spaced floorboards to the shivering family upstairs. Low and oppressive, the four downstairs rooms retain mangers and stone-paved floors. The long room to the side, a rabbit hutch and chicken coop, is mostly a pile of fallen stone. *"Volumi,"* Fulvio says, that magic word, *volumes,* which can be translated into square meters and presented to the town architects for additional space in these tightly controlled historic buildings. He is sizing up how much will have to be excavated, and how that will affect the foundation. The upstairs four rooms are high-ceilinged and possess two fireplaces and a worn stone sink under a window. One room has traces of decorative painting on the pitted and falling plaster. All the windows look over the treetops at the silhouette of Cortona nestled on the distant spur of Sant' Egidio. We see the volcanic cone of Monte Amiata drawn in outline above the horizon, surrounded by the rippling Apennines. What you hear is—silence. The first rains have opened the torrent and its light music sounds like an extension of silence. Fulvio tells us he never has restored a house for anyone before. He prefers big projects of his own.

The next day we go to lunch with Fulvio and Aurora at Mondo X in Cetona. They were married at this eleventh-century cloister, which is a recovery residence for people with drug problems. These reforming young people operate a restaurant fit for the heavenly host. The restoration, which Fulvio considers one of the best in Italy, was also accomplished by the residents. We're wild about the food and ambiance, which manages to feel both luxurious and chaste. At the end of a long succession of dazzling courses—each presented with Zen clarity—Fulvio raises his glass. "Because you are friends, I would like to be involved in the project. To my opinion, we will have a lot of work."

We place ourselves under Fulvio's tutelage. The three of us make many site visits, deciding where the stairs will come down, which rooms will be bathrooms, where the brooms will be stored. We are to locate the builder for the structures and roof. Fulvio will supervise, then later supply the artisans for the finishing work and cabinetry. "Down there, just out of sight, we will have a beautiful pool." I almost can see it in the pupils of his eyes, instead of the actual snarls of broom and weed trees.

And so we begin a new saga of restoration. This time we will not be doing the work ourselves, but we are in charge of overseeing the work and finding authentic materials as they are needed.

Fulvio surveys the first project, the roof of flat, rounded, lichen-etched, overlapping stones. "These old roofs requiring restoration must be regarded as art objects," he says. As each stone is removed and stacked, some break. Rotted beams are ripped out, then the chimneys are stabilized and insulated. This laborious process is only two sentences long; the work takes a year. First, the walls of the hay barn and the long chicken coop room must be rebuilt. Then we realize that we are short quite a few square meters of stone. We begin running all over the countryside, often with our builder, Danilo. We visit every stone pile in this part of Tuscany. All building supply lots keep a stash of grapestones, old brick, capstones, beams, well covers, roof tiles,

HISTORIC RESTORATION
OF CEILING

LOOKING INTO THE RESTORED
KITCHEN; TRADITIONAL "CAT EXIT"
WINDOW OF ANTIQUE BRICK

HAYBARN RISING

FONTE DELLE FOGLIE'S
COLLAPSED CHICKEN
HOUSE, WHOSE DESTINY
IS A KITCHEN

and plain old stone. Every builder and stonemason hoards these private collections. Because they love stone, they're loathe to sell.

Danilo is resourceful. From a convent in Montepulciano, he obtains a beam that three hundred years ago must have been the mightiest tree in Tuscany. He finds five-foot-long steps when two of ours break as they are being reset. Our gardener, Fabio, has a friend who has dismantled a shed. We buy a trunkful of roof stones from him. Our original builder at Bramasole, Primo Bianchi, lives in a maze of materials he's gathered. Danilo loads his truck there. We locate another cache in Monte San Savino. At other places we find no roof stones, but we uncover other timeworn treasures. One by one, we discover stone door and window surrounds, hefty square paving stones for constructing the *marciapiede,* the sloping "sidewalk" for drainage around the house. The great treasures are the eight-foot-tall grapestones, which we can use to build an iron-hooped pergola of instant beauty. We buy a curved stone from which water someday might fall. Someday. Like Primo, we, too, now have our own squirrelly stockpile.

But we did not have enough stones for the hay barn roof. *Il maestro* steps in. Fulvio has a load of new stone delivered, and along with it plastic vats usually used in wine-making. The next day several kegs of chemicals arrive. "We will dip each stone in potassium permeate. *Invecchiato,* it's called. To make old. It dries for half an hour and then each stone is rinsed."

"Every stone individually?" Ed, I can tell, is thinking of the man-hours required.

"Absolutely. Then they look mottled. They are worked in with the original stone so they are not noticeable."

That night at dinner, Ed and I contemplate the process. "We wanted a historic restoration," I remind him.

"The stock market is going south," he says. "This *will* be a good investment." By morning, we've convinced ourselves that having roof stones, hand-dipped like fine chocolates, is just what we want to do.

Not only is the roof a work of art, the rest of the house is too. As I write today, we are finishing this entire project. Egisto, where are you? We need the iron chimney fittings and the tiny windows. The past few weeks have been the most challenging of all because everything is coming together. The windows must go in before the beams can be finished. The beams must be finished before the floors are sealed and waxed. The painting must happen after the floors. The outside tubes must be installed and covered before the stones are laid around the house. And on and on. We spend a month coordinating all the players—engineer, *geometra,* electrician, plumber, black-smith, painter, on and on. We're going mad. Friends we take to see the house say, "You're brave," and we know they mean we are balmy. At this point, Ed just wants the freedom to get up in the morning and study the past anterior tense in Italian.

The rains come, and the trenches around the property, which look like the Battle of the Somme, literally run with water. The excavation for the gas and water tanks behind the house becomes unstable. We are horrified at little landslides. Truckload after truckload of sand pours into the ditches. Elio, with his gigantic earth mover, slides whole hillsides back and forth as numerous pipes and tubes fit together. We're waiting for the electrical company to take down their hideous concrete poles so the wires can be buried. Our troop of Bramasole stonemasons begins to rebuild the fallen walls and to clear brush. We're also waiting for Fabio's cousin to top trees so the view is opened to a wider span. No matter where we are, Ed is on the phone, putting one person in touch with another. Fulvio loses his temper with a couple of the men. Danilo shrugs and quotes Archimedes, who said *give me a lever and I'll move the world.* Ed marvels that he knows the writings of the Greeks, as well as Etruscan and Roman history, the way to make *vin santo,* and all of Shakespeare. I only wish the information coming our way did not stop all the workers, who listen attentively for as long as Danilo holds forth.

At dinner each night, we try to remind each other why we are doing this. "We're not going to live there. We thought we were making a wise business move."

"Yes, but you love it out there. The investment took a turn of its own. Everyone in the family can enjoy it. We can give it to friends. To an artist or writer for a month."

I lamely quote Yeats, "In dreams begin responsibilities." But then I realize that with Fonte, that's backward. A responsible land investment, instead, turned into a dream. Now we have it right in the middle of our lives. After a bottle of Riccardo's Ardito, we remember how lovely the air is in the mountains, what a joy to gather wild strawberries, violets, chestnuts, and porcini. The workers rave over sweet, sweet grapes that bolted into the oaks. We remember the feral apple trees, how crunchy and tart the gnarly fruit tastes on fall walks. After every big rain, waterfalls appear, great shunts of fresh falling water and, suddenly, frogs singing, *neap, neap.* And working with Fulvio has taught us the rigors of good restoration. Our standards are forever altered and our consciousness about what is excellent forever changed. His insistence on fine-tuning brings his outstanding results. More than once we were shocked to hear, "Take it down. Do it again." When the men rebuilt the exterior kitchen walls, Fulvio had them insert many small pieces of stone in the cracks, along with bits of broken terra-cotta. That's the way the original walls were built. Side by side with the old, his new version is even more textured. When we finish the house, it will look very much as it did when we first glimpsed the ruin through the scrim of blackberry bushes. But it will be warm in winter, with heating under the *cotto* floors. The septic system exits down the hill with water you could drink (no thanks). The well goes down 130 meters, where, finally, an aquifer was struck and the holiest of waters surged for three days.

We scour the countryside for a stone fireplace. Ed requests a kitchen fireplace for grilling. Danilo builds one with brick and a small beam. For the other downstairs fireplace, in what Fulvio refers to as a cozy music room for winter, we finally come upon a small stone one in Le Ville. With a rampant lion—symbol of Cortona—carved under the mantel, it seems right at home where the old sheep manger once was. Upstairs, the grand fireplace where the farmers cooked waits only for its metal chimney liner and damper. Then Francesco will plaster the top, and the sagging old beam will be replaced. Not perfectly straight across, but slightly akilter, the way we found it. Only Fulvio would think to replace it imperfectly.

Sauro lays out various brick patterns for us to choose among. Fulvio suggests a simple squared-off pattern for the downstairs because it was traditional in stables. For the upstairs, I choose the pattern the farm wife might have selected, the more refined herringbone. Bruno finds seven pairs of three-hundred-year-old doors for the outside. They're terribly expensive, we groan. Fulvio prices new doors. They're less. He says, "Up to you. But you've gone this far." Needless to say . . .

We search for old chestnut flooring, since the original upstairs had floors from the trees on the land. *Cotto,* the cooked brick, is traditional in Tuscany, except this far into the country where the woodcutters and shepherds lived. Old stone is easier to find than old wood. But Beppe remembers dancing on a wooden floor in the house in his youth. For twenty-five years, he worked as the count's shepherd and lived in one of the now-abandoned houses near the villa. He's told us about the years when he and his wife, Beppina, made pecorino and ricotta. The echoes of their steps become important to us. I envision sitting in the living room, imagining them restored to youth, waltzing.

Then Bruno calls. Through a friend, he has located floorboards from the Teatro Signorelli in Cortona. Replaced seventy years ago, they've been in storage. He has enough for the living room. We rush down to his shop in Camucia. He swipes beeswax down the grain of one board. The thick wood is worn to a patina similar to an antique dining-room table. Again, Fulvio says, "My goodness."

Bruno then finds stairs from the eighteenth century. The risers are rabbeted smartly into the sides. He sets it against a wall for me to try. Five steps up, I turn around and suddenly remember that I will wear high heels. I will crack my ankle on these steep, narrow steps. That detail of historical restoration will have to be sacrificed to fashion. We're thrilled to get the call when Bruno also discovers venerable interior doors someone lavished polish on for a couple of centuries. But should we? We're over budget—but still well under a moderately nice small condo in California. We say yes.

By affirming the handmade, Fulvio retains the intangible feeling of warmth and character that draws us to old houses. We come to see that the quality we value in food, wine, furniture, fabrics, and gardens is all of a piece with the restoration. The hassle is big but the satisfaction immeasurable.

When I tell Fulvio what I would like for the kitchen cabinets, he laughs. I knew he would love the detail. Since the long kitchen once was a chicken coop, I ask for cabinets with chicken wire in the doors. Lucani, the local artist, is poised to work in several rooms. As further homage to the original purpose of the downstairs, he will paint the eight panels of a double door with medallions, each one featuring a sheep, rabbit, cow, or ox, the house's oldest inhabitants.

The kitchen will be filled with baskets, another homage. On my first visit to Fonte with Fulvio, a man who resembled a spirit suddenly emerged from behind the hay barn. The dog accompanying him, half as tall as this

ANGELO WITH HIS BASKETS

elfin man, seemed mythic, too. They embodied the spirit of the mountain. We met Angelo, shy and hard of hearing, who wanders the mountain gathering reeds, sticks, willows, and vines. In his mountaintop aerie he weaves baskets that have great soul. My first gift to Fulvio was one of Angelo's baskets. He makes some with whittled sticks with little branches to hook over the handle and over the limb of a tree, so you hang it easily while you pick plums or cherries. Though he is not a hermit, he reminds me of those followers of St. Francis.

By spring, all the restoration subplots will begin. We will be moving furniture inside. Then the landscaping starts. Cosimo de' Medici, what to do with several acres where wild boar tear up the ground and snort under the windows every night? No marble mythological creatures, no mighty waterworks, no embroidered parterres here. We'll just go with a fairy-ring of golden apple trees, lots of rosemary, hawthorn, and miles of wild roses. On the slope down to the torrent, which used to be a potato field, Ed wants an orchard of all the fruit trees. The collapsed bread oven will be rebuilt outside the kitchen and a pergola beside it. Our friends will come here to swim and roast guinea hens and potatoes. Ed's sisters' families and my nieces and nephews will come for the olive harvest. My daughter may someday write a book here. Our grandchild, Willie, will grow up catching crayfish in the stream, picking up chestnuts in the fall, and hiding in dense woods. At twenty-one months, he already says *buon giorno, buona notte, ciao, cappuccino, espresso, fuori, acqua,* and *dopo.* He especially loves *dopo.*

Dopo, later. We project this future for our house. But, of course, you never know what will transpire. You do know that if you have the power to restore a piece of local history, you've saved something. The philosophy is intrinsic to the Tuscan way of life. *To restore: to bring back, to put back, to give back.* I like the last definition. Casa Fonte delle Foglie has looked out into these hills for almost a thousand years. Now the house fills with new life.

MICHELANGELO, BEPPE, PIERO, ARMANDO, BUILDERS OF DRY STONE WALLS AT FONTE DELLE FOGLIE

MONDO X, CETONA

FULVIO'S BAROLO RISOTTO

RISOTTO AL BAROLO DI FULVIO

Fulvio's favorite Barolos are Marchesi di Barolo, Fratelli Barale, Villa Sebaste, Brezza, Bergadano, and Gaja. The cook deserves a glass, too.

1 SHALLOT, MINCED
4 TABLESPOONS OLIVE OIL
2 CUPS RISO SUPERFINO CARNAROLI (HE RECOMMENDS TENUTA CASTELLO) OR ARBORIO RICE
1 BOTTLE BAROLO
6 CUPS VEGETABLE STOCK, TO WHICH IS ADDED A VEAL BONE
1 BEEF BOUILLON CUBE
1 CUP GRATED *PARMIGIANO*
NUTMEG
1 TABLESPOON MINCED FRESH CORIANDER
PEPPER

Sauté the shallot in the olive oil for 2 minutes. Add the Riso Superfino Carnaroli and continue to sauté for a couple of minutes more, then add a cup of the Barolo, bring to a boil to evaporate the alcohol, and reduce heat to a simmer. Meanwhile, in another pot, heat the stock. Ladle the stock gradually into the rice, alternating with a cup of Barolo. Allow the liquid to be absorbed before adding more. After ten minutes, add one beef bouillon cube and the marrow from the veal bone. After another five minutes, before the rice is al dente, add the last of the Barolo. A minute before you remove the risotto from the heat, add ½ cup of the *parmigiano,* a shaving of nutmeg, the coriander, and pepper. Let rest for 2 to 3 minutes. Serve and pass a bowl of the remaining *parmigiano.*

SERVES 4 AS A MAIN COURSE OR 8 AS A FIRST COURSE.

Butta la Pasta!

THROW IN THE PASTA!

Just after we returned to California from Italy last winter, I saw Ed take the seldom-used scales from the pantry and weigh the potatoes and flour for the gnocchi he was making. He jotted a few notes on a pad. Late in the afternoon, when I came downstairs, I saw trays of gnocchi. He'd prepared three versions. At that moment, I knew he'd turned pro on me. "This time," he said, patting the puffy pillows, "I'm going to find out whether I can re-create the same tastes here." Although we've been cooking with great pleasure under the Tuscan sun for years, we've often lamented that the tried-and-true chicken with olives, basic *ragù,* eggplant *parmigiana,* and other everyday favorites at Bramasole just don't soar at our California table.

All summer, Ed had cooked in Tuscany. When our friend and assistant, the lovely Giuseppina, came over to help, he took notes and asked her a thousand questions. She's a young mother of two boys, who lives in a *casa colonica,* traditional stone farmhouse, far in the country with her husband and his parents. Their family feasts initiated us into the eight-hour meals so common in the Tuscan countryside.

12

PIATTO DEL GIORNO
RIBOLLITA
PICI AL RAGÙ TOSCANO
PICI ALL'AGLIONE
RAVIOLI AL LIMONE
TAGLIOLINI AL TARTUFO

PROSCIUTTO E MELONE
INSALATA CAPRESE

TRIPPA ALLA TOSCANA
FILETTO DI MANZO AL TARTUFO
FILETTI DI MAIALE AL VINO
FILETTI DI MAIALE ALL'ACETO
BRACIOLE ALLA GRIGLIA
SALSICCE ALLA GRIGLIA

FRANCES AND FRIENDS OUTSIDE
TRATTORIA TOSCANA IN CORTONA

Without a glance at a recipe, Giuseppina, like so many of our friends here, simply knows how to cook. Under scrutiny, however, Ed discovered that she had quite a few habits and techniques so native to her skill that she never bothered to mention them when she gave us a recipe or explained how she'd made something. We love everything she cooks. Sometimes when we're working on a project, we ask her to prepare a dinner for friends. The best request—"Surprise us." Often we cook together. She's intrigued by my desserts and preparation of vegetables. I'm interested in everything she throws in the pan.

While I worked upstairs on designs for my furniture collection and a book, Ed sharpened his knives. Giusi taught him to make *tulipani,* curved tulip-shaped cookie cups filled with fresh fruit. She showed him the intricacies of cutting up rabbit and soaking *cinghiale,* wild boar, in vinegar. On his mornings alone, he worked in the vegetable garden before the heat, then I'd hear Evora or Jovanotti singing and know I'd find a treat when I came downstairs to lunch after staring at the computer for hours. He invented his own artichoke-stuffed veal rolls, baked sea bass stuffed with capers and parsley, rabbit with raisins and *vin santo.*

When he worked on his manuscripts, I shopped and cooked in the afternoon—desserts and delicate *sformati* of flavorful vegetables. We especially like the terrines of *ceci* (chickpeas) and ones of zucchini with mint and lemon. *Sformati* means unmolded, the *s* working like the *a* in English—as in *atypical.* I varied a classic and came up with a summer dessert we adored—white peaches stuffed with almonds in a mixture of mascarpone and cream. At night when we cooked together, Ed started bossing me around in the kitchen, correcting the way I minced, adding seasonings after I'd already seasoned, subtly consigning me to the butcher-block cart while he manned the stove.

I said nothing. As a woman who had made probably twenty thousand dinners in this life, I'm ecstatic that this hungry man has fallen in love with everything from Artichokes to Zucchini flowers. Both of those, in fact, reaped compliments from

Giusi. Ed's batter resulted in the crispest, tastiest fried artichokes and zucchini flowers I've ever tasted. Both Giusi and I stood by the stove marveling. Is there a greater joy than a man who cooks?

He'd always enjoyed the kitchen. He wrote poems about cooking to music. He plied me with cookbooks on my birthday. When he shopped in San Francisco, he came home with lingonberry jam, salted plums, kumquats, grapeseed oil. In Tuscany, he'd find truffle butter, artisan rice, *lardo,* tiny lentils. He always had his specialties— cheese soufflé, chicken with forty cloves, sea bass in salt crust, and his mother's graham cracker pie. He cooked to Jussi Björling arias, Buddha-Bar, Portuguese fado, "Rainy Night in Georgia," and Penguin Club. "What music goes with the quail with juniper berries?" He's nuts. "A little Bebel Gilberto?" Odd, but the airy music seems to lift the aromas of the quail quietly simmering in pancetta and a dash of *vin santo,* sending them through the house.

He stocks our California larder with canned organic tomatoes for oven roasting, with balsamic vinegars of different ages, artisan risottos, along with all the small treats we bring home in our luggage: pine nuts, capers, *ceci* (chickpeas), *farro,* dried *funghi porcini,* cubes of the porcini bouillon, tubes of *gianduia* (hazelnut chocolate), and of truffle paste, cannellini beans, a big can of anchovies, stone-ground polenta, Umbrian lentils, biscotti from Prato, and boxes of exquisite candies, almost too pretty to open. Many of these things are now available through gourmet shops here, but in Tuscany any little grocery store's shelves provide these tasty souvenirs.

Ed found that keeping generous supplies from Tuscany depressurizes cooking. At the wave of a wand we can eat *pasta al pomodoro,* pasta with tomatoes, which is soul food, or a saffron and *parmigiano* risotto, cooked the way Venetians like it, *all'onda,* with a creamy wave.

Soon after his transformation from dilettante into pro, he started to pump up every BTU possible to bring to our California home the essences of our Tuscan

PECORINO (EWE'S MILK
CHEESES) FROM PIENZA

ED'S FRIED ARTICHOKES

CINTA SENESE PIG, A ONCE RARE BREED OF BELTED PIG, NOW RAISED AGAIN IN TUSCANY

BRINGING TUSCANY HOME

kitchen. We have always been astonished at how easily friends in Italy seem to produce a dinner for ten. Partly, that's because Italian food is simple. Few ingredients comprise each dish, and the ingredients are top quality. The first revelation from our friends? Food focuses celebration. Thanks to these friends who have shared hundreds of dinners with us, and thanks to their *trucs,* Tuscany came home to California quite naturally. Ed's Marin County minestrone may be even better than the one we make at Bramasole. His secret weapons for the soup are his slow-roasted oven tomatoes and his homemade chicken stock. He makes a batch every week. My daughter loves best the *melanzane alla parmigiana,* the rich layered eggplant, which Ed made ten times before he finally watched every step of Giusi's process. Two eureka moments came when he saw her peel the eggplant and then when he saw that she quickly fried each floured slice in a *lot* of sunflower oil. Because the oil is so hot, the eggplant doesn't absorb; it just sizzles. His *ragù* perks away on the back burner for three hours. It's so good you just want to hula. This is everyday food. Served with that essential local characteristic, generosity, it is the heart of the Tuscan way of life. Family and guests, pull up a chair—the platters are arriving.

The challenge for those who like to eat well will always be the random Monday or Wednesday night. We used to find party cooking fun but weekday dinners sometimes a drudge. We came home from work at seven and only wanted a frittata or takeout. If I were alone, sometimes I'd eat ice cream with a fork on the back porch and go to bed. How to eat well on a daily basis? How to treat yourself well? Don't you deserve it? Gradually, we have learned the wisdom of the famous call that mammas all over Italy receive regularly from returning husbands and children as they round the bend, *butta la pasta,* throw in the pasta. When the one of us working stands up wide-eyed from a desk littered with papers, the other is salting the water, bringing it to a boil.

Our California pantry is well stocked with extra virgin olive oil, that cornerstone Tuscan ingredient. Despite wide availability now, olive oil is the most misunderstood

GIUSEPPINA DE PALMA, "GIUSI"

ED MAKES GNOCCI

aspect of Italian cooking. A grasp of the Tuscan way with oil revolutionizes your kitchen. Use oil liberally. The least obese people in the fifty-one countries of Europe, Italians don't measure out the oil in teaspoons. With robust food, wine, and a habit of daily walks, the people of Italy also have the best longevity in Europe and the lowest suicide rate—no one wants to leave the table. With food so good, everyone practices moderation quite naturally. Because of American food schizo-phrenia, food fascists and faddists in America are legion. They should be confined to a diet of mung beans. Oil is the immortal ingredient. To obtain the *true* taste of Tuscany, tip that oil bottle forty-five degrees! "Olive oil does not make you fat," Silvano, the hardware store owner in Cortona, assures us. He and his wife are lean and sound.

"How much do you use?" Ed asked.

"A minimum of a liter of oil a week for the two of us." Beppe and Beppina use a gallon a month. In their seventies, they have splashed a ton of oil on their pasta over the years. Intrigued, Ed asks all our friends. This liter a week is typical. Giuseppina takes off our little dribbling spout and pours straight from the bottle.

I'm always appalled when food writers advise using something resembling motor oil (if only they knew the milling process) for cooking, while saving the extra virgin oil only for salads. That's nonsense. Good oil imparts an upbeat flavor with a kick. I frequently see people on the return flight to the U.S. hand-carrying a bag filled with bottles of oil. *Bravi!*

If you ever visit an olive oil mill during the harvest, you'll always buy the best oil you can find. From year to year, our oil's taste varies. This drought year's oil sets a record for spiciness. A late spring freeze killed many of the delicate olive flowers, resulting in a tiny crop that produced intensely green and flavorful oil, peppery with a slight almond fragrance. The aftertaste tingles. Generally, the earlier you pick, the more piquant the taste, while late oil is full and mellow. Either, when just pressed, has a deep freshness and purity. After the first pressing, quality starts to slide down the bell curve. Some of the expensive oils I see for sale in the United States I would not use on a rusty hinge. They're too old and they're blends from the nether regions. As for "light oil"—please! It has the same calories and is overrefined. Select your oil as carefully as you select perfume. First look for the label's date of best use. Even in great cookware stores, unfortunately, you can pick up three-year-old oil. At its best within eighteen months of when the olives were picked and pressed, oil will remain excellent for six more months or even longer, especially if stored in a dark bottle out of sunlight. We were tasting several local oils with Giancarlo at the mill where we bottle ours. "I want you to try something," he said, and pulled a bottle from a box under a table. The gold color revealed that it was not this year's oil, but we were stunned when he threw down his cap and laughed. "Unique, no? I pressed this oil in 1974." The oil was thirty years old! Kept in a dark, cool corner of the mill, it retained the distinct taste of olive oil. We would not cook with it, but neither of us detected anything rancid or "off." He then poured another oil that was fusty and mildewed. "Sat in a sunny window *one week*," he explained. "Now this next one is 100 percent *pendolino* olives from the Val di Chio . . ."

Before buying oil, check for the government's DOP (Denominazione di Origine Protetta) or IGP (Indicazione Geografica Protetta) marks, which guarantee the product as pure Tuscan. Some oils may be packaged to appear Tuscan, but actually are mixes from Tunisia, Spain, or the South of Italy. Those regions, of course, have their own good oils, but inferior grades, blended in bulk, definitely suffer. For deep frying, select another oil. Tuscans use peanut or sunflower.

As soon as we return to California from Italy, we want avocados, salsa, Thai food, burritos, rich desserts—all the flavors we've missed. In a week, we're back to shopping for Martelli dried pasta, stirring the Sardinian *fregula* pasta, and slow-roasting a loin of pork. We are definitely pouring our own extra virgin olive oil into every pan. Italian food is good every day. As our neighbor, Placido, says, "We've tried it all. The tagines and sushi, the Chinese and Mexican. We prefer Italian." We come back to it as the earthiest, most fun to cook, and healthiest food. We brought home, too, the rhythm of the Tuscan meal: *antipasto, primo, secondo, dolce*—the dinner of four symphonic movements. The sequence of courses promotes leisure and conversation. No one dish outweighs the other. No plate is laden. You're presented, family style, with a series of tastes to be savored separately, a balletic balance of colors and aromas. This ease of Tuscan dining is a portable concept.

For years Ed was my sous-chef. Now I'm his. We no longer have to speculate to each other about why the pasta doesn't taste the same—because of the water or the flour or the phase of the moon. We make our own, or search for artisan dried pastas. We're regulars at the cheese shop. We have our sources staked out. Most importantly, we've adjusted the recipes to compensate for certain disadvantages to cooking in the United States. For example, we use more garlic and herbs here because their flavor is not as intense. The farmers' market helps, too. Ed believes in going early. At one grower's stand last week, he found one bunch of *puntarelle,* a type of chicory Romans love. Seeking organic local food is a must. Growing herbs—what a simple bonus. In more isolated places, the Internet can be your friend—cheeses, flours, coffees, wild boar, anything is available, even in the heart of the Mojave. Ed's recipes that we love to make together—anywhere in the world—follow, along with his kitchen notes.

ZUCCHINI FLOWERS FROM BRAMASOLE'S GARDEN

Le Ricette di Edoardo

ED'S RECIPES

"*Nostrano,*" Nunziatina at the *frutta e verdura* says, and I know that I'm going home with a sack of the Lago Trasimeno peas or the delicate beans she's holding in her hand. *Nostrano,* meaning "our own," signifies that her mother or husband shepherded these particular delectable vegetables into this world. "*Genuino,*" Beppe calls anything he pulls up from our garden, or the rabbit dripping blood that he gives us to roast. The rabbit has fed on cuttings from our garden and leftover bread. I'd like to paint those two watchwords above my kitchen door. The best things are *nostrano.* I hope they have the *genuino* gene attached to them as well. Luckily for me, the passion for cooking hit me in Tuscany. I trained myself there, with a little help from Frances and friends—quite a bit of help, actually. With such ingredients, cooking always seems fun and easy. Back in the States, I relish the long Saturday mornings in the kitchen. Later in the week, I might wander in for an afternoon and try something challenging, or maybe a dessert. Having lived for twenty-five years in the Bay Area crucible of food revolution, I feel honor-bound to tweak classic recipes if I get the urge.

I start my Saturday cooking marathons just as I do in Tuscany, by gathering herbs—thyme, rosemary, oregano, basil, and parsley. I rinse, dry, and finely chop them separately, reducing what was a handful to a quarter cup or less. I keep each in a separate jar, then use these seasonings throughout the morning of cooking.

Then I'm ready to start peeling garlic and running a couple of sheets of tomatoes into the oven for a nice slow roasting. Next, I set artichokes on to steam, throw the chopped *odori* (the mix of onions, carrots, celery, and parsley they give you in the *frutta e verdura*) into the oil for my *soffritto*—now I'm rolling, ready to launch into filling my jars, then I'll start my first major plate of the day.

These jars sustain us. With them, a pasta sauce is at the ready, as is a platter of anti-pasti. A snack after the movie takes five minutes, and for lunch, a spoon of roasted garlic or artichoke pesto turns a sandwich into an event. A bowl of soup seems blessed by a spoon of basil pesto. Frances grows enough basil for a platoon, so we always have her bags of pesto made in ice-cube trays crowded into the freezer until I finally throw them out. We make a mint pesto in the summer, too, which is snappy with shrimp for a quick pasta. This stocking the fridge with jars, besides being handy, looks so fine when they're lined up on a shelf—an illusion that all's right with the world.

To all my recipes, add your own salt or pepper. I don't always use them. Olive oil means extra virgin oil, as fresh as possible. Again, use your discretion. Italian recipes use the sensible abbreviation *q.b., quanto basta,* meaning whatever is enough.

Ed's Jars

A basic tenet of my new kitchen philosophy is the concept of jars. Our neighbor Fiorella has on hand her big *barattoli,* jars, of tomatoes from the summer garden, dried mushrooms from the fall hunts, jams for tarts, and all kinds of vegetables *sott'aceto,* preserved under vinegar. Because Fiorella and Placido are the truest *buongustai* we know, I adapted their idea to our two kitchens. We've found that the whole idea shifted the work in the kitchen to a different level. It's fun to spend a morning preparing artichoke pesto, roasted garlic, tomato sauce, then filling the jars. With good basics on hand, what we cook the rest of the week seems effortless. Most of my jars will keep a week in the fridge.

[149]

BRINGING TUSCANY HOME

SOFFRITTO

This basis of Tuscan cooking has no translation into English (*mirepoix* in France is sautéed more gently.) The simple *soffritto,* literally "fried under (oil)," is fried *odori*: onion, carrot, celery, and parsley. One can add a variety of other ingredients to change the tastes, though Tuscans don't: a few minced cloves of garlic, a quarter pound of minced pancetta, four or five minced basil leaves, or other aromatic herbs. Use this in *ragù,* soups, and as a seasoning for zucchini, peas, or other vegetables. Mix with bread crumbs and stuff tomatoes with it. On and on. When I add a cup of oven-roasted tomatoes and run the mixture through a food mill, I can serve forth a perfect *sugo* for Sunday-night spaghetti. Double or triple this to have more on hand.

4 TABLESPOONS OLIVE OIL TO BEGIN
SOFFRITTO: 1 EACH: CARROT, ONION, CELERY STALK, ALL MINCED
HANDFUL OF PARSLEY, MINCED

※ Sauté—no, fry—the ingredients in a 4-quart saucepan until they begin to color, about 7 to 10 minutes. Add more oil if the mixture seems too dry.

MAKES 1 CUP

TOMATO SAUCE
POMMAROLA

Pommarola—classic, essential, ubiquitous. For true fast food: one-quarter cup *pommarola* per person, stirred into pasta, a wave over the plate with *parmigiano,* and *èccolo!* This is the food for which homesick Italian expatriates or travellers yearn. Some even travel with *pelati,* cans of Italian tomatoes, so they can whip up a meal redolent of home. I chop the tomatoes with a hand blender, right in the pan or can.

¼ CUP OLIVE OIL
1 SMALL ONION, MINCED
ONE 28-OUNCE CAN WHOLE PEELED TOMATOES, COARSELY CHOPPED
½ CUP CHOPPED BASIL LEAVES

※ In a 4-quart saucepan, sauté onion in oil for 3 to 4 minutes on low heat. Add the tomatoes, salt to taste, and basil. Turn to medium heat and cook, uncovered, for 10 minutes.

MAKES 3 CUPS

OVEN-ROASTED TOMATOES
POMODORI AL FORNO

This is your ace. We make these all summer long with fresh tomatoes, but it's also excellent with canned tomatoes. I use Muir Glen Organic. You also can use halved cherry tomatoes. The slow roasting concentrates the flavors of the herbs, oils, and tomatoes. Throw it together in a flash, then you get to smell the rich aromas deepening through the morning, while you move on to something else. Keep on hand in jars, dipping into them when you want to enrich a soup or use as the start for a pasta sauce with roasted vegetables or shrimp or sautéed eggplant. The plump little darlings garnish a roast or, chopped, wake up a risotto. To make a spread, purée the roasted tomatoes in a food mill and stir in 3 to 4 tablespoons of olive oil. If you scatter a tablespoon of red pepper flakes over the tomatoes while they're cooking, you'll have a spicy spread. Or, for a savory variation, add a couple of tablespoons of roasted garlic or *soffritto* to the purée.

THREE 28-OUNCE CANS OF WHOLE PEELED TOMATOES, DRAINED, CUT IN HALF LENGTHWISE
¼ CUP OLIVE OIL
3 TABLESPOONS EACH MINCED FRESH ROSEMARY, THYME, OREGANO, BASIL
5 GARLIC CLOVES, CHOPPED
SALT AND PEPPER

☀ Preheat the oven to 200° F.

☀ Arrange the tomatoes cut side up on a jellyroll pan. Drizzle the oil and scatter herbs and garlic over them. Salt and pepper to taste. Bake for 2 hours.

MAKES 3 CUPS

ARTICHOKE PESTO
PESTO DI CARCIOFI

8 MEDIUM ARTICHOKES
3 GARLIC CLOVES, MINCED
ZEST AND JUICE OF ONE LEMON
¼ CUP OLIVE OIL
½ CUP GRATED *PARMIGIANO*
PINCH OF SALT

 Cut the top two-thirds off each artichoke, strip off the grungy leaves, and steam the artichokes until barely tender, about 15 minutes. When cool enough, remove the rest of the leaves and the choke. Place the hearts with the other ingredients in the food processor and pulse until almost smooth. Leave a little texture. You may need more oil, depending on the size of the hearts.

MAKES ABOUT 2 CUPS

OLIVE SALSA
SALSA DI OLIVE

1 CUP PITTED GREEN OR BLACK OLIVES
2 TABLESPOONS SALTED CAPERS, RINSED, THEN SOAKED IN COLD WATER FOR 5 MINUTES AND DRAINED
2–3 GARLIC CLOVES
3–4 TABLESPOONS OLIVE OIL
1 TABLESPOON FRESH THYME

 In a food processor, chop the first three ingredients, then add the oil and thyme and whirl a couple of times.

MAKES ABOUT 1 CUP

TUSCAN BEANS AND SAGE
FAGIOLI E SALVIA

1 POUND DRIED CANNELLINI BEANS, SOAKED FOR 6 TO 7 HOURS,
    THEN SIMMERED UNTIL BARELY TENDER
OLIVE OIL
7–8 SAGE LEAVES, CHOPPED
SALT AND PEPPER

 Purée the beans with enough olive oil to make a spread.
Add sage and season to taste.

MAKES 3 CUPS

GRILLED RED RADICCHIO
RADICCHIO ROSSO AI FERRI

Mix this into a salad or serve alone in "cups" of whole red radicchio leaves.

6 SMALL HEADS OF RED RADICCHIO
3–4 TABLESPOONS OLIVE OIL
3 SLICES OF PROSCIUTTO, DICED

 Cut 5 of the radicchio heads in two and put facedown on a grill for a few minutes. Turn and grill the other side. When cool, chop, douse with oil, and combine with the prosciutto. Carefully remove the leaves from the remaining head of radicchio and spoon the grilled radicchio into the "cups."

SERVES 4

ROASTED GARLIC
AGLIO AL FORNO

As a variation, toast one quarter-cup of walnuts. Chop and stir into the garlic purée. Spread on bread or crackers or use to flavor whatever needs a hit. While the rest of the jars will keep a week, plan to use the garlic within two or three days.

4–5 WHOLE HEADS OF GARLIC
7 TABLESPOONS OLIVE OIL
SALT

* Preheat the oven to 250° F.

* Choose healthy and firm bulbs. Cut the top ½ inch off the heads to expose the cloves. Place in a covered baking dish and pour oil onto each. Roast for 45 minutes or longer, depending on the size of the heads. When cooled, squeeze out the pulp into a bowl. Whirl briefly in a food processor with salt and a little more oil, if needed.

MAKES ABOUT 1 CUP

BAKED OLIVES WITH GARLIC AND CITRUS ZEST
OLIVE AL FORNO CON BUCCIA DI AGRUMI E AGLIO

A welcome twist on a bowl of olives served with drinks. Serve warm or at room temperature.

2 CUPS MIXED OLIVES
4 GARLIC CLOVES
1 TABLESPOON OLIVE OIL
1 TABLESPOON RED WINE
ZEST OF 1 ORANGE AND 1 LEMON
A FEW FLECKS OF DRIED RED PEPPER
½ TEASPOON CHOPPED FRESH OREGANO

* Preheat the oven to 300° F.

* Mix all the ingredients and bake in an earthenware dish for 15 minutes.

MAKES ABOUT 2 CUPS

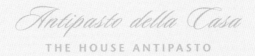
Antipasto della Casa

THE HOUSE ANTIPASTO

A trattoria menu always lists *antipasto della casa*. I order it because the chef can showcase what's fresh and what's on his mind. It will include prosciutto, several *salumi, crostini neri* (rounds of bread with a chicken liver spread), two or three other crostini, artichoke hearts, melon, and other things the chef fancies, perhaps beef tongue or fresh *alici* (sardines). For the crostini, use thin slices of a baguette. In Tuscany a special loaf called a *stinco*, shinbone, is sold especially for crostini at every *forno*.

At home in California, when Frances and I cook together for friends we find that festive platters of antipasti around the kitchen, along with that first good bottle of Querciabella Chianti Classico, get the dinner off to a nice warm start. Or we make a huge platter and pass it at the table. By far, numero uno at our casa is fried zucchini flowers. At I Tre Bicchieri restaurant in Arezzo, I learned to stuff them with potatoes and basil, which accentuates the crunchy flowers.

In addition to the above trattoria list, we up the amps to the antipasto platter by adding:

- Spears of roasted asparagus. Oven roast asparagus drizzled with oil at 400° F. until barely tender.
- Crostini of red peppers. Slice and "melt" peppers with balsamic vinegar in a frying pan on low heat for half an hour.
- Crostini of roasted garlic and walnuts
- Crostini of grilled radicchio (page 153)
- Crostini with beans and sage (page 153)
- Big capers with stems attached
- Three or four kinds of olives

OSTERIA DEL TEATRO OWNER, EMILIANO ROSSI,
AND HIS FIANCÉE, YLENIA LANDUCCI WITH THEIR
ANTIPASTO DELLA CASA

FARRO SALAD
INSALATA DI FARRO

1 POUND *FARRO*

¼ CUP *SOFFRITTO* (PAGE 150)

½ CUP OLIVE OIL

¼ CUP PINE NUTS

ZEST AND JUICE OF 1 LEMON

1 CUP HALVED CHERRY TOMATOES

CHOICE OF ARUGULA LEAVES, PEAS, *FAVE*, OR MINT, *Q.B.*, AS YOU LIKE

1 TEASPOON FRESH THYME

SALT AND PEPPER

RADICCHIO OR LITTLE GEM LETTUCE LEAVES

☀ Wash and cook 1 pound of *farro* with 8 cups of water or chicken stock (like rice) for about 20 minutes. The *farro* should retain a little bite.

☀ Mix everything except the radicchio together. Season with salt and pepper to taste, and serve on the antipasto platter, spooned into curls of radicchio or Little Gem lettuce leaves. Like tabbouleh or wheat berry salads, *farro* can come to the table as a first course, lunch, or salad.

SERVES 8

FRIED ZUCCHINI FLOWERS
STUFFED WITH POTATOES AND BASIL
FIORI FRITTI

You can use the same batter for *carciofi fritti,* fried artichokes. Use tiny artichokes, cleaning off all the hard leaves. Thinly slice, dip in batter, and fry. Tuscans also love to eat early spring artichokes raw, finely sliced.

2 RUSSET POTATOES, PEELED, STEAMED, AND RICED
2 TABLESPOONS BUTTER
¼ CUP HOT MILK
10 BASIL LEAVES, CHOPPED
25 ZUCCHINI FLOWERS, BLOTTED WITH A TOWEL, BUT NOT WASHED
PEANUT OIL FOR FRYING
1 CUP ALL-PURPOSE FLOUR
1 CUP BEER, OR MORE IF NEEDED
SALT

Mix the hot potatoes with butter and milk, then add the basil. Gently pull open each zucchini flower, then reach in, snap off the stamen, and discard it. You can leave the flower stem attached. With a spoon, form about a tablespoon of potato into a lozenge shape and insert it in the flower. Pinch the top of the petals together. In a large frying pan, add oil to about 1 inch depth and set over medium-high heat.

In a medium bowl, mix the flour and beer until you've formed a thin but not too watery mixture.

Test the oil with a pinch of flour. If it quickly sizzles, the oil is ready. Dip each flower into the batter, then lower into the oil. Don't overcrowd the pan. With tongs or a fork, turn each flower over after 2 to 3 minutes. When the flowers stop "talking," after another 2 to 3 minutes, transfer them to paper towels to drain and salt them. Serve immediately.

MAKES 25 FLOWERS

Primi

Like the Tuscans, I want pasta every day. Italians eat sixty pounds per person every year. That's one and a quarter pounds a week and, at a quarter pound per serving, that's five servings of pasta a week. Those with fear of flour should take a tour around any Italian piazza, where people are looking good. For a festa, our friends often serve a *tris* of pastas, a trio, such as *cavatelli* with *ragù,* tagliatelle with mushrooms, and ravioli with four cheeses. We have fun preparing farfalle with shrimp and mint pesto, *orecchiette* with broccoli and pancetta, penne with eggplant. Hundreds of pastas are 1-2-3 simple. Sometimes we make something more splendiferous.

SHRIMP IN PASTA SHELLS
WITH THREE CHEESES
GAMBERI IN CONCHIGLIE CON TRE FORMAGGI

Frances was honored with an award from Barilla Pasta, and she invented this recipe for the ceremony dinner, using Barilla Jumbo Shells. I make it also with Pasta di Gragnano's *Lumaconi*, which means big snail shells. In Italy, they're commonly called *conchiglie*, conch. These pasta shells, when topped with shrimp, to echo the sea, may provoke a round of applause when you bring them to the table.

1 POUND (ABOUT 24) MEDIUM SHRIMP

OLIVE OIL AS NEEDED

SALT AND PEPPER

24 LARGE PASTA SHELLS

2 EGGS

⅓ CUP GRATED *PARMIGIANO*

1 POUND RICOTTA

1½ CUPS GRATED MOZZARELLA

1 TABLESPOON ROASTED GARLIC, OR 1 TEASPOON MINCED FRESH GARLIC

4 TABLESPOONS CHOPPED BASIL LEAVES, PLUS WHOLE LEAVES FOR GARNISH

JUICE OF 1 LEMON

1 CUP TOASTED COARSE BREAD CRUMBS

3 TOMATOES, CHOPPED

※ Preheat the oven to 350°F.

※ Peel the shrimp and sauté in a little olive oil until barely done. Season with salt and pepper.

※ Cook the pasta according to package directions, adding a teaspoon of salt to the water and taking care not to overcook. Cook a few extra shells in case of breakage. Drain and carefully toss with a spoonful of oil in a bowl. Set aside.

- Combine the eggs with the three cheeses, garlic, and half of the basil. With a teaspoon, stuff each shell with the cheese mixture. Arrange in a large oiled baking dish. Press one shrimp onto each. Mix the lemon juice with 2 tablespoons oil and moisten the shells. Sprinkle bread crumbs on top. Bake for 15 minutes.

- Prepare tomato coulis: Cook the chopped tomatoes very briefly in a little oil. Add the remaining basil at the end.

- Serve the shells on a pool of tomato coulis and garnish with basil leaves.

- For a main course, sauté more shrimp and surround the shells on the plate with four or five more.

SERVES 8 AS A FIRST COURSE

PICI WITH FRESH FAVA BEANS, CHERRY TOMATOES, AND AROMATIC HERBS

PICI CON FAVE FRESCHE, POMODORINI, ED ERBETTE

Pici is Cortona's favorite pasta. Mine, too. Silvia Regi of Il Falconiere taught us to make the long strands three or four times the thickness of spaghetti. At Trattoria Toscana, Santo serves it *all'aglione*, with lots of garlic and bread crumbs. Debora and Arnaldo, at Pane e Vino, serve *pici* with anchovies and bread crumbs. When *pici* is on the menu, I can go no farther. Silvia invented this recipe for her restaurant, and her addition of *fave* is typical of her touch. Tuscans have been saying *fave* since 1221. Those beans Jack planted were inevitably *fave*—the only bean Europe had before the great culinary heists from the Americas began. A good wine for this *pici* is Isole e Olena's Syrah. If you would like a white, try Tenimenti Luigi D'Alessandro Cortona Fontarca.

FOR THE PASTA
2 CUPS FLOUR
1 TABLESPOON OLIVE OIL
PINCH OF SALT

FOR THE SAUCE
8 TABLESPOONS OLIVE OIL
2 GARLIC CLOVES, CHOPPED
2 CUPS CHERRY TOMATOES, QUARTERED
SALT AND PEPPER
½ CUP FRESH *FAVE* BEANS, STEAMED UNTIL BARELY DONE
2 TABLESPOONS MINCED AROMATIC HERBS
½ CUP BREAD CRUMBS
½ CUP GRATED PECORINO CHEESE

To make the pasta: Mound the flour on a board and make a well in the center. Into the well add 5 tablespoons water, oil, and salt and slowly mix in the flour, adding more water from time to time as the dough comes together. You are aiming for a soft but not sticky mix, but don't worry if the dough is stiff, as it will relax while it rests. Form the dough into a ball, cover loosely with a dish cloth, and set aside for 20 minutes.

❄ Cut the dough into very thin pieces. Roll each piece into a snake about the thickness of a chopstick and about 2 feet long. Continue until all the dough has been cut and rolled.

❄ To make the sauce: Heat about 6 tablespoons of the olive oil over medium-high heat in a saucepan. Add the chopped garlic and sauté until the garlic is soft but not brown. Add the cherry tomatoes and salt and pepper. Cook rapidly, stirring occasionally. Add the *fave,* then the aromatic herbs. Transfer the mixture to a bowl. In the same pan, add the rest of the olive oil and bread crumbs and sauté until lightly browned.

❄ Meanwhile, bring a large pot of lightly salted water to a rolling boil and drop in the *pici.* Boil until they rise to the top, then remove them with a slotted skimmer and transfer into the pan with the olive oil and fried bread crumbs. Briefly sauté the mixture, then add the *fave* mixture. Add a handful of grated, aged pecorino cheese. Serve immediately.

SERVES 4

{165}

POTATO GNOCCHI

GNOCCHI DI PATATE

I love making gnocchi. What a pleasure to crowd the counter with little nubbins about to be boiled and smothered with sauce. At some point in the fall, Beppe digs up all that's left of the potatoes in the vegetable garden and spreads them out on a bed of straw in the *limonaia*. They'll keep all winter long, becoming perfect for gnocchi as they develop more starch than newer russets. I bake the potatoes in a jellyroll pan, to which I add a half-inch layer of rock salt.

Gnocchi are most tender when served immediately. If you're serving the gnocchi several hours later, put the just-cooked and drained gnocchi into a bowl of cold water, and let them sit for a few minutes. Drain them, drizzle with olive oil, and put in a sealed bowl in the refrigerator. You can reheat them in sauce in a frying pan, or mix the gnocchi with the sauce and heat in a 350°F. oven for 10 minutes. I suggest pouring everyone some San Felice Chianti Classico Poggio Rosso Riserva.

4 POUNDS (ABOUT 8 MEDIUM) RUSSET POTATOES
1 TABLESPOON SALT
1½–2 CUPS UNBLEACHED ALL-PURPOSE FLOUR

* Bake the potatoes in a 350°F. oven for 1 hour. Let cool slightly. Peel and put potatoes through a ricer. Add salt. On a flat surface, mound the flour, make a well, and heap the potatoes in the center. Mix with your hands until the dough starts to come together. Knead for several minutes, then form into an 8-inch-long roll. Cut the roll into quarters, then take one quarter and roll it in your floured hands. Put it on the floured work surface and continue to roll it, as if your fingers and palms were rolling pins. The dough will lengthen, becoming three or four times longer. It should be about ½ inch thick. Cut into little "knuckles," and dust with flour if they're at all sticky. Repeat with the rest of the dough.

* Drop a third of the gnocchi into boiling salted water. Cover to bring the water back to a boil. Check in the next 2 minutes to see if the gnocchi are starting to float to the top. When that happens, they're done. Remove with a slotted spoon and add another batch to the boiling water. Since the potatoes are already cooked, you're really only cooking the flour. Add cooked and drained gnocchi to a frying pan of sauce, coat them, and serve.

SERVES 6

MEAT SAUCE FOR GNOCCHI
RAGÙ DI CARNE

This is the definitive *ragù di carne.* Every Tuscan eats this on tagliatelle from the age of six months until the day of death.

½ CUP OLIVE OIL
1 CARROT, FINELY MINCED
1 ONION, FINELY MINCED
1 STALK CELERY, WITH LEAVES, FINELY MINCED
HANDFUL OF PARSLEY, FINELY MINCED
1 POUND GROUND BEEF
2 PORK SAUSAGES, REMOVED FROM CASING
SALT AND PEPPER
1 CUP RED WINE
ONE 28-OUNCE CAN WHOLE PEELED TOMATOES, COARSELY CHOPPED
1 TABLESPOON TOMATO PASTE

* Prepare a *soffritto* with the 4 tablespoons oil, carrot, onion, celery, and parsley (see page 150), and reserve.

* In a 4-quart heavy pot with a lid, add the rest of the oil and sauté the ground beef and sausages until browned. Add salt, pepper, and the red wine. After the wine has almost all evaporated, add the *soffritto,* tomatoes, and tomato paste. Partially cover and simmer over a very low flame for 3 hours, stirring now and then. If the sauce looks too thick, add a shot of water.

SERVES 8

PASTA WITH PANCETTA
PASTA AL FUMO

If *pancetta affumicata*, Italian smoked bacon, is not available, use regular bacon. That stash of tomato sauce made on Saturday sends this Monday night pasta quickly to the table. The smooth Rocca delle Macie would be good to pour with this pasta.

1½ POUNDS PENNE

4 TABLESPOONS OLIVE OIL

1 GARLIC CLOVE, MINCED

1 SPRIG ROSEMARY

½ POUND *PANCETTA AFFUMICATA*, DICED OR GROUND (IF GROUND, IT BONDS
    BETTER WITH THE PASTA)

2 TABLESPOONS WHITE WINE

2 TABLESPOONS TOMATO PASTE

1 CUP TOMATO SAUCE (PAGE 150)

2 TABLESPOONS HEAVY CREAM

Bring a pot of salted water to a boil, then add penne. Cook until al dente and drain.

Heat the oil in a saucepan over medium heat and add the garlic and rosemary, sautéing until the garlic colors slightly, 3 to 5 minutes. Discard the garlic and the rosemary. Add the pancetta to the oil but don't salt it. Cook for 5 to 10 minutes, then add the white wine. Add the tomato paste and the tomato sauce, cook another 5 minutes. Add 2 to 3 tablespoons water if the sauce is too dense. Cook for another 10 minutes, then add the heavy cream. Mix with the penne and serve. Always reserve some pasta water in case your sauce needs thinning.

SERVES 6

FIORELLA'S BLACK CABBAGE SOUP
ZUPPA DI CAVOLO NERO DI FIORELLA

What to have on Ash Wednesday, the beginning of Lent? At the table of our neighbors, the Cardinali, after Fat Tuesday, *martedì grasso,* we sit down to black cabbage soup. When Fiorella told me how to make the soup, I realized that the whole turns out to be so much more than the sum of its ingredients. I said, *"Water? Twelve cups of water?" La cucina povera,* the poor kitchen, is the source of many of Tuscany's tastiest dishes. At this prelude to Lent, Chiara tops some crostini with sliced cherry tomatoes and a slice of *mozzarella di bufala,* buffalo milk mozzarella, and runs them under the broiler for a moment. After the soup, Fiorella brings out a plate of anchovies and capers and a big bowl of the soft cheese, *stracchino,* and we help ourselves.

3 POUNDS *CAVOLO NERO,* BLACK KALE, WASHED, LEAVES ONLY, CUT INTO 3-INCH PIECES
10 THIN SLICES OF RUSTIC BREAD
1 GARLIC CLOVE, PEELED
10 GARLIC CLOVES, MINCED
OLIVE OIL AS NEEDED
SALT AND PEPPER

* Boil the kale in water to cover for ½ hour. Meanwhile, toast the bread on both sides under the broiler and rub generously with the garlic clove. Try using a fork to hold the garlic if the clove is too small.

* Layer the bottom of a large serving bowl with a few slices of bread, sprinkle a little of the minced garlic over them, and spoon out a layer of the kale with some of its broth. Season with salt and pepper. Continue adding the layers and broth. Serve with a cruet of good oil.

SERVES 10

THE BIG VEGETABLE SOUP
MINESTRONE

Winter's favorite song. Even better the next day, when you can turn this minestrone into a *ribollita* by adding hunks of country bread as you reheat it.

3 ONIONS, CHOPPED

3 CARROTS, CHOPPED

3 CELERY STALKS WITH LEAVES, CHOPPED

HANDFUL OF FLAT-LEAF PARSLEY

⅓ CUP OLIVE OIL

HANDFUL OF FRESH THYME

1 BUNCH RED OR GREEN CHARD, CHOPPED

8 CUPS CHICKEN STOCK

1 CUP WHITE OR RED WINE

ONE 28-OUNCE CAN WHOLE PEELED TOMATOES, CHOPPED

3 TABLESPOONS TOMATO PASTE

1 CUP OVEN-ROASTED TOMATOES (SEE PAGE 151)

HEEL OF A WEDGE OF *PARMIGIANO*

3 POTATOES, PEELED, CUBED, AND STEAMED

1 CUP COOKED CANNELLINI BEANS

SALT AND PEPPER

In a large stockpot, sauté the first four ingredients in the olive oil for 5 minutes. Add the thyme and chard and mix. Then add the stock, wine, and the tomatoes, tomato paste, and oven-roasted tomatoes and bring to a near boil. Throw in the heel of *parmigiano,* then reduce the heat to low so the soup barely bubbles for 45 minutes. Add the potatoes and beans. Salt and pepper to taste.

SERVES 12

EGGPLANT PARMESAN

MELANZANE ALLA PARMIGIANA

This is the most tested recipe in the book. I went on a quest to duplicate, exactly, the savory miracle Giusi always leaves in our kitchen on the day we arrive. I varied the amount and kinds of oil, peeled the eggplants and tomatoes or didn't. We decided—Giusi agrees—this one is the best. I recommend a few glasses of Ciacci Piccolomini's Rosso di Montalcino Fonte.

3 MEDIUM EGGPLANTS, PEELED AND THINLY SLICED
FLOUR FOR DREDGING
2 CUPS SUNFLOWER OIL
SALT
2 CUPS TOMATO SAUCE (PAGE 150)
HANDFUL OF FRESH BASIL, ABOUT ¼ CUP, TORN INTO PIECES
4 OUNCES *PARMIGIANO*, GRATED
8 OUNCES MOZZARELLA, GRATED

❉ Preheat the oven to 350°F.

❉ Lightly dredge the eggplant slices in the flour, shaking off excess, and fry them in batches in sizzling sunflower oil until lightly browned. Drain on paper towels and salt them.

❉ Spoon some tomato sauce on the bottom of a 9 x 12-inch baking dish. Add a layer of eggplant, then a layer of tomato sauce, a few basil leaves, and sprinkle some *parmigiano* and mozzarella. Add another layer of eggplant, sauce, and basil, finishing with *parmigiano* and mozzarella on top.

❉ Bake for 45 minutes.

SERVES 6

CHICKEN WITH OLIVES AND TOMATOES
POLLO CON OLIVE E POMODORI

This is good served with a polenta made with a lot of *parmigiano* and a glass of Sette Ponti's Crognolo.

5 TABLESPOONS OLIVE OIL
1 WHOLE CHICKEN, CUT IN 8 PIECES, LIGHTLY DREDGED IN FLOUR
½ CUP RED WINE
1 CUP PITTED MIXED BLACK AND GREEN OLIVES
6 TABLESPOONS CHOPPED FLAT-LEAF PARSLEY
1 CUP CHOPPED OVEN-ROASTED TOMATOES (PAGE 151)

❋ Preheat the oven to 350°F.

❋ Heat the oil in a large frying pan and brown the chicken pieces, 3 to 5 minutes per side. Add the wine and transfer to a baking dish. Mix the remaining ingredients, pour over the chicken, and bake uncovered for 30 to 45 minutes, depending on the size of the pieces, turning the chicken once.

SERVES 4

ROLLED VEAL SCALLOPS
STUFFED WITH ARTICHOKES

INVOLTINI DI SCALOPPINE CON CARCIOFI

Beppe lined the back of our vegetable garden with artichoke plants. We've grown to love the silvery green leaves along the terrace. Artichokes we overlook dry on their stalks then transform into brilliant blue thistles, which we cut and mix with wildflowers. We've now experimented with artichokes as much as with rampant zucchini. For this recipe, I put two of my favorite ingredients together. When you serve it, open a full-bodied Merlot: try Vignalta's Colli Euganei Rosso Gemola, a wine from the area southwest of Padua and Venice, near where the fourteenth-century poet Petrarch lived at the end of his life. I think a line or two of his poetry melted into the grapes.

FOR THE FILLING

12 (ABOUT 1½ POUNDS) SMALL ARTICHOKES
¼ CUP OLIVE OIL
½ RED ONION, MINCED
2 GARLIC CLOVES, MINCED
1 CUP BREAD CRUMBS
3 TABLESPOONS MASCARPONE (SEE NOTE)
1 EGG, BEATEN

FOR THE VEAL

8 (2 POUNDS) VEAL SCALLOPS
¼ CUP OLIVE OIL
FLOUR FOR DREDGING
1 CUP RED WINE
1 CUP CHICKEN STOCK
1 CUP HEAVY CREAM

To make the filling: Steam the artichokes until just tender, about 15 minutes. Strip off the outer leaves until you reach the palest green leaves. Leave the soft leaves but remove the thistle, if there is one. Chop coarsely by hand. In a medium skillet, heat the oil and sauté the onion and garlic for 2 minutes, then add the artichokes and continue cooking for another 2 minutes. Add the bread crumbs and cook 2 minutes. Remove from the heat. When the mixture is cool, add the mascarpone and the egg. Stir well.

☀ Have your butcher pound the veal scallops quite thin or flatten them yourself between layers of plastic wrap with a pounder. Lay out all 8 pieces of veal on a work surface and put a heaping tablespoon of the artichoke mixture on each. Spread with a spatula, then roll up and tie with string. Heat the oil in a skillet. When hot, dredge the veal rolls in flour and add to the skillet. Sauté 2 minutes on each side, turning them with tongs. Remove to a plate and cover to keep warm.

☀ Add the wine and chicken stock to the skillet and boil vigorously for 10 minutes. Remove from the heat and add all of the cream, allowing it to meld gently into the liquid. Return to heat and continue boiling for another 5 minutes until sauce has begun to reduce and thicken.

☀ You can serve the veal "birds" whole, but for a nicer presentation, remove the string, slice each rolled scallop into ½-inch-thick slices and arrange them in a fan shape on individual plates. Spoon sauce over top.

SERVES 8

NOTE: In the U.S., where mascarpone is usually rubbery, I prefer to use crème fraîche. They're not the same thing but work equally well in some recipes.

ROLLED SOLE WITH FENNEL AND CITRUS
INVOLTINI DI SOGLIOLA CON FINOCCHIO E AGRUMI

Every year we grow more and more fennel. We also harvest the wild fennel flowers, dry them, and keep them all year to sprinkle on oven-roasted potatoes. Let me count the ways. Baked fennel couldn't be better. You simply cut six or seven fennel bulbs in eighths, steam them until barely tender, spread them in a well-buttered oven-proof dish, dot the fennel with more butter, and add a layer of grated *parmigiano*. Run the dish into the oven and bake for about 20 minutes at 350°F. I first discovered a version of this in the Florence airport restaurant!

A winter salad of thinly sliced fennel, minced shallot, blood orange sections, and crisp, pungent lettuces keeps the taste buds quite happy. Feathery fennel plumes add a flourish to any plate and are more interesting than parsley or a sprig of rosemary. Snip them over a salad, or encircle a platter of roast chicken with the wands. Fennel marries well with fish, as we see below. The citrus finish of Il Palagio's Sauvignon works well with the sole.

1 FENNEL BULB, DICED
1 TEASPOON FENNEL FLOWERS OR SEEDS
1 GARLIC CLOVE, MINCED
1 ORANGE, PEELED, SECTIONED, AND DICED
ZEST AND JUICE OF 1 ORANGE AND 1 LEMON
1 CUP TOASTED BREAD CRUMBS
6 FILLETS OF PETRALE SOLE
OLIVE OIL, AS NEEDED
½ CUP WHITE WINE
2 TABLESPOONS CHOPPED FENNEL FRONDS (OR PARSLEY)

Preheat the oven to 350°F.

Sauté the diced fennel briefly, until barely tender, add fennel flowers or seeds, then the garlic just for a final minute. Add the orange sections and the zest of the orange and the lemon (reserving some for garnish). Add two-thirds of the bread crumbs.

Wash and dry the fish fillets. Top each with a layer of the fennel mixture. Gently roll up the fillets. Drizzle with oil and ¼ cup of the wine, sprinkle with the remaining bread crumbs and bake for 20 minutes.

❋ In a small saucepan on top of the stove, blend the juices of the lemon and orange and the remaining ¼ cup of wine. Bring to a boil, then reduce heat to a simmer and let the sauce reduce for 10 minutes.

❋ Remove fish to a platter and stir juices from fish dish into the citrus juice mixture. Spoon the sauce on top of the fish and garnish with zests and fennel fronds.

SERVES 6

WHITE PEACHES WITH ALMOND CREAM
PESCHE BIANCHE CON PANNA DI MANDORLA

Frances's first choice for a summer dessert, perhaps because it takes her back to her Georgia childhood. The presentation looks like what the angels eat, but the taste is rich.

FILLING

1 CUP MASCARPONE (OR CRÈME FRAÎCHE, SEE NOTE ON PAGE 177)
JUICE OF ½ LEMON
¼ CUP HEAVY CREAM
¼ CUP SUPERFINE SUGAR
½ CUP SLICED ALMONDS, TOASTED AND COOLED
1½ CUPS CRUSHED ALMOND COOKIE CRUMBS, SUCH AS AMARETTI

6 LARGE WHITE PEACHES, RIPE BUT NOT SOFT
1 CUP WHITE WINE OR CHAMPAGNE
2 TABLESPOONS GRANULATED SUGAR
MINT LEAVES FOR GARNISH

❋ Mix all the filling ingredients and chill for 15 minutes.

❋ Peel the peaches and halve them, removing the pit. Bring the wine and sugar to a boil in a medium saucepan, add the peach halves and poach for 3 to 4 minutes, frequently spooning liquid over the halves. Remove the peaches from the liquid and cool.

❋ Spoon a mound of the mascarpone mixture into the center of the peach. Serve, garnished with mint leaves.

SERVES 6

TULIP SHELLS WITH THREE BERRIES

TULIPANI

I watched Giusi make tulip-shaped cookie shells for a party. She filled them with strawberries and cream. The next day I ventured into pastry, previously totally Frances's territory. I made a fall version with sautéed pears, whipped cream, and cinnamon. With leftover batter, I improvised crisp, silver-dollar-sized cookies, adding a few sliced almonds to each. A small glass of fragrant Moscato di Pantelleria served with *tulipani* will bring dinner to a mellow finish.

FOR THE 8 TULIPS

½ POUND BUTTER (2 STICKS)

1¾ CUPS CONFECTIONERS' SUGAR

4 EGG WHITES

1¾ CUPS FLOUR

FOR THE FILLING

4 CUPS MIXED BLACKBERRIES, RASPBERRIES, AND STRAWBERRIES
   (AND ADD PEACHES IF YOU LIKE)

4 TABLESPOONS BROWN SUGAR

1 CUP MASCARPONE (OR CRÈME FRAÎCHE, SEE NOTE ON PAGE 177)

5 TABLESPOONS GRANULATED SUGAR

1 CUP HEAVY CREAM, WHIPPED

THIN PEEL OF 1 LEMON OR ORANGE

⁂ Preheat the oven to 350°F.

⁂ To make the *tulipani*: Melt the butter in a medium-sized saucepan. Remove from the heat and add the sugar and mix. Whisk in the egg whites, mixing well. Add the flour and stir until the batter forms ribbons. On a cookie sheet, butter two 7- to 8-inch circles. Spoon some batter on each circle and spread very thinly with the back of a spoon. It will look like a crêpe. Repeat on a second sheet. Bake for 8 to 10 minutes until slightly browned, checking often.

⁂ Lift off a circle with a spatula. Immediately place it on a kitchen towel that you're holding in your hand. Gently press the bottom of a 2-inch-diameter glass into the center of the circle, forming a tulip-like shell. Quickly, the tulip will harden enough to handle. Put aside to cool. Repeat with the others.

⁂ Make the other 4 *tulipani*.

⁂ When all the *tulipani* are completely cool, put them in a bowl or on a plate and cover with plastic wrap, otherwise the *tulipani* will become soft. They will keep two days this way.

⁂ To make the filling: Mix the berries with the brown sugar.

⁂ Beat together the mascarpone with 3 tablespoons of the sugar and half of the whipped cream, which has been sweetened with the remaining 2 tablespoons of sugar. Spoon this into the shells and top with the fruit. Then top with dollops of the remaining whipped cream. Garnish with citrus peel.

SERVES 8

Un Grappolo d'Uva

✳

A BUNCH OF GRAPES

When we bought Bramasole, we found every room stacked with dusty wine bottles. Each one housed a scorpion or spider. We hoped to find coin silver spoons, sepia photographs, or perhaps a locket with a curl of baby hair inside. Instead, we hauled away stacks of newspapers, crumbling olive nets, and cascading, crashing loads of bottles. "Those people must have been carousing for decades," I complained. The land was so overgrown that we did not even know a vineyard had once thrived on our hills. We uncovered a few sculptural grapestones, used for training the vines out over the terrace edge. As we hacked evil weeds and brambles, we found stunted, knotty remains of vines still surviving after thirty years of abandonment. Ed and Beppe began to prune and tie them to wires they strung between the grapestones.

Finally, three years ago, we made our first wine. Beppe brought over the traditional chestnut container, and we smashed the grapes with a dowel and our fists, then left the luscious mush to ferment. Beppe took over the ancient task of making the *contadino* (farm) wine.

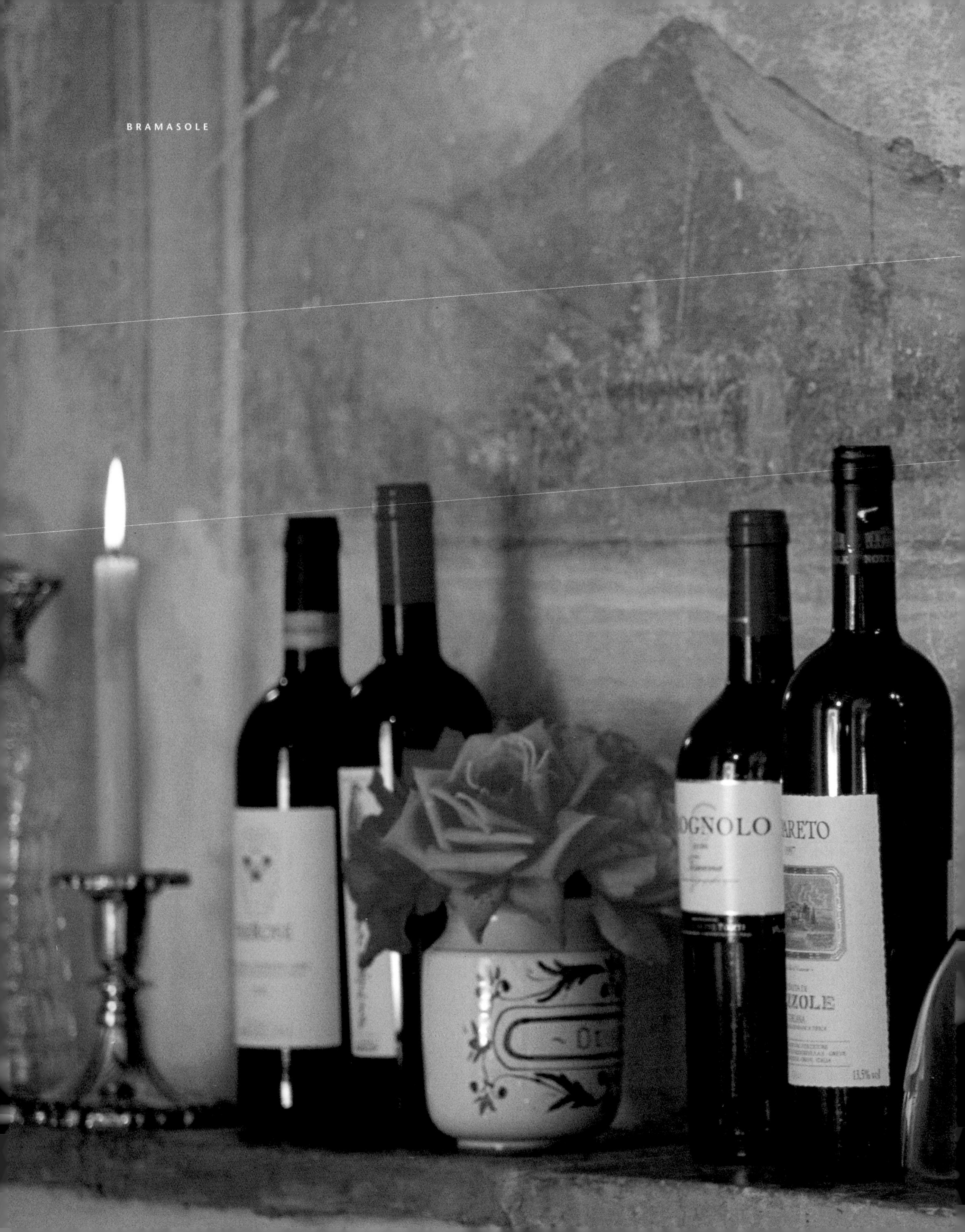
OGNOLO
ARETO
ZOLE
13,5% vol

MARCO MOLESINI AT
HIS CORTONA ENOTECA

When we came back several months later, we found twelve bottles of our own wine in the kitchen. We were thrilled. I mentioned designing a label. We invited four close friends over for a ceremonial opening, and Ed and I cooked all day. Ravioli with four cheeses and tomato sauce, a slow-roasted pork loin with garlic, our garden's tiny potatoes, baked fennel, and an apple-almond tart. We served Prosecco with baked olives and our own roasted almonds in the living room before dinner, and so were already festive when we gathered at the table. Ed opened the wine and splashed it into our gigantic Brunello glasses. We toasted. To the gods of wine. *In vino veritas.* Live forever. *Salute.* We all tasted. I saw Cinzia pull in her lips. The expression on her face made me think she had beeen stung by a scorpion. Carlo's eyebrows hit his hairline. The wine was . . . The wine was—oh, no—the *worst* I've ever tasted.

We had made our Bramasole wine with an unholy mix of whatever grapes grew on our property. Perhaps that explained its full-in-the-mouth taste of shoe polish, its finish of dusty walnut shells and mildewed grass.

"How many bottles?" Franco asked tactfully.

"Twelve," Ed said. Then he laughed. "I think we have eleven too many." He gathered the glasses and took them to the sink. "Dust unto dust." He poured the deceptively gorgeous claret liquid down the drain and returned with two bottles of firmer repute.

Almost thirty years ago, a blink in Tuscan time, hidebound winemaking traditions began to change. Growers started to plant what Ed calls the red trinity—cabernet sauvignon, merlot, and syrah—foreign grape varieties, in addition to the region's revered sangiovese. Previously, *quantity* had been the standard. Most of those old-style mass-produced wines sent me straight to the aspirin bottle. A glass of white Vernaccia or Trebbiano gave me a headache just to look at it. Although exceptional reds always came out of Tuscany, the area produced a plethora of rough-and-ready Chiantis

LEFT GRAPES ARE CRUSHED IN TRADITIONAL TORCHIA *ABOVE MIDDLE* WINE
WORKERS AT IL FALCONIERE'S VINEYARD: CLAUDIO MONALDI AND EMANUELE
BERNARDINI

in straw (later woven plastic) covered bottles. Sometimes the chemicals could blister
your lip, and the murky-around-the-edges color was reminiscent of ox blood.

Simultaneously with the planting of new grapes, growers began to update their
agricultural and technical methods. As the cabernet sauvignon, merlot, and syrah
vines went into the ground, so did other almost-lost stock. As the world knows, the
result was the new Super Tuscans, which sounds closer to a puffed-up soccer team
than to great wine. *Super Tuscans* is an unfortunate nomenclature because nothing is
revealed or exalted by this name. Regardless, the wines began to muscle into the shelf
space previously dedicated to the great Tuscan Brunellos, Vino Nobile di
Montepulcianos, and Chiantis.

Over the past decade, we've reveled in not only these stellar Super Tuscans, but
also the enormous improvement in the other traditional wines. Even Brunello, made
entirely of brunello grapes, a local name for sangiovese, improved through the
advancements. The new methods carried over into *all* of Tuscan winemaking—
dense planting, hard pruning, and the use of small, mostly French *barriques* for
aging, instead of trailer-sized barrels. The culling of green grapes in early summer was
the toughest lesson of all, for the result is a dramatic reduction in *quantity* and a need
to go on faith that the result will be a dramatic increase in concentration and *quality*.

Part of the problem for Chianti wines in the 1960s was that wineries were per-
mitted to use up to 30 percent white grapes. In 1984, however, the Denominazione

di Origine Controllata (DOC) committee reduced the requirement of white grapes to 2 percent and allowed certain other grapes—cabernet and merlot—to make up 10 percent of the volume. Finally, in 1996, the regulations opened to the reality of change already underway; oenologists finally were allowed to eliminate white grapes completely. The renegade trinity grapes could make up 15 percent of the volume. At this point, an odd and confusing twist occurred: a Chianti is now a Super Tuscan—if it so desires. Just as surprising is that some excellent Chiantis are now 100 percent pure sangiovese. A Chianti can be nearly anything it wants to be.

Super Tuscans came about as winemakers rebelled against the outmoded laws regulating Chianti production. By adding the red trinity to sangiovese, they had to risk going with the lowbrow designation *vino da tavola,* plain old table wine, since their wines didn't fit the government's DOC and DOCG (Denominazione di Origine Controllata e Garantita) appellation regulations. But they raised the *vino* to the power of ten. By now, we have a specific designation for these wines that don't conform to DOC or DOCG regulations: IGT (Indicazione Geografica Tipica). Winemakers may experiment with different blends and still maintain high standards. For a full explanation of the baroque Italian government designations, see the Italian Trade Commission website: www.italianmade.com.

These laws are why the Chianti you drink now is a world away from the ones you first tasted. To anyone who says, "I don't like Chianti," as I once said, open two or three new-style Chiantis and prepare for her to be flummoxed: those from Castello di Volpaia, Marchesi de' Frescobaldi, Castello di Fonterutoli, and Castello di Querceto are four of hundreds of marvelous wines on the move to greatness.

Riccardo Baracchi, a close friend, exemplifies the new Tuscan winemaker. In early June we walked through his vineyard with him just after the green grapes had been cut. Only a few *grappoli* were left on each vine. The sacrificed greens lay strewn on the ground. He showed us his spacious new *cantina*, gesturing from the terrace at an olive grove he plans to transplant. He will replant the field with vines. He has just bought more Cortona land and plans to make a white wine. Since Cortona became a DOC zone in 1999, suddenly the area has become one of the primo wine districts. With plantings of the red trinity, plus chardonnay, sauvignon, and pinot nero grapes, Cortona has leapt from a zone of drinkable, casual wines to distinguishable bottlings from Baracchi, Trerose, La Calonica, Avignonesi, and Tenimenti Luigi d' Alessandro.

Riccardo first started his vineyard only six years ago. He's a hands-on vintner, working in jeans and boots with his men. We were there when he planted the slopes below Il Falconiere, the inn he and his wife, Silvia, own, with cabernet sauvignon, syrah, merlot, and sangiovese. In 2003, he released his first Super Tuscan, called Baracchi Ardito. He gave the world forty-five hundred bottles of this 2001 vintage. At the same time, he released eight thousand bottles of an affable second wine, Rosso Smeriglio, made up of equal parts of sangiovese, syrah, and merlot.

We came for dinner the night he opened the first bottle of Ardito. Riccardo looked movie-star handsome in his pale gray suit. "Not even my mother has tasted this wine," he told us. "I took it to Vinitaly in Verona in April. My little wine didn't get much notice at first, but then lots of people started coming over. Then in a blind tasting by *Wine Spectator,* it scored a ninety-three!" The exuberance of his wine matches his personality. Like its maker, a glass of Ardito brims full of laughter and wit.

The recent wines from Bolgheri, in western Tuscany, already are legendary—wines such as Tenuta San Guido's Sassicaia and Tenuta dell'Ornellaia's Ornellaia and Masseto are benchmark wines. The Maremma area, vicinity of Grosetto, also is a rising star with its Moris Farms Avvoltore and Le Pupille's Morellino di Scansano and Saffredi. Close to Arezzo, youthful wines are reaping top marks for Sette Ponti, named for the seven bridges between Arezzo and Florence. At lunch with owner

Antonio Moretti, we drank a 1998 Crognolo, his first release, with the antipasti. He also is an exemplar of the new Tuscan wine culture. Until 1997, the vineyard, formerly a hunting estate for Antonio's father, sold all the grapes on the property. That year, new vines, with the help of an oenologist, a viticulturalist, and an agronomist, plus the vision of Antonio, transformed the vast estate into one of the most exciting vineyards in the country.

The table was vast, the courses plentiful. The Crognolo is a strapping, sexy wine, as hearty as the food. Then Antonio poured his Oreno, and the conversation momentarily died. Whoa! At that moment, we didn't know this wine's summa cum laude destiny—only that it seemed like liquid lyric poetry.

All over Tuscany this is happening. We've "grown up" with our local Avignonesi and Poliziano vineyards over the past decade as they've achieved world-class status for their Vino Nobile di Montepulciano and other wines. Boscarelli, another old friend, we've been happy to cheer on as it climbed the big charts. A glance at a list of the recent great vintage years (1995, 1997, 1999, 2000, 2001) shows one hit after another. New grapes, new laws, new methods converge. The 2003 crop promises stellar releases. Future vintages of Tuscan wine will continue to dazzle us year after year.

Tuscans regard wine as food. This is a major cultural difference—a healthy one. They don't sit around drinking wine—they drink as they eat. Although a few friends might serve a Prosecco before dinner, most invite you to the table soon after you arrive. They skip the cocktail hour, when the palate is dulled by alcohol. At the table, of course, wine flows. When dessert exits the kitchen, no one seems to touch the wine again. (I miss the long last glass as the evening tapers.) At that point, local grappa and *vin santo* travel around the table, or perhaps an exquisite Moscato from Pantelleria, or a Moscadello from Montalcino. The stumpy Tuscan cigars come out, too. A few smokers light up, but most now have the grace to step outside—a definite improvement.

ABOVE LEFT ANTONIO MORETTI OF SETTE PONTI ABOVE RIGHT BENEDETTO BARACCHI BELOW (LEFT TO RIGHT) ARNALDO ROSSI, SILVIA REGI, RICCARDO BERTOCCI, BENEDETTO BARACCHI, RICCARDO BARACCHI AT IL FALCONIERE, CORTONA

BRINGING TUSCANY HOME

With all the new boomtown mentality for wines, we wonder if the traditional wine-as-food philosophy will erode. Wine tastings are becoming common, although so far, copious platters of food accompany each wine. I've noticed that the number of bottles I haul out after guests leave is about half that of a California dinner party. This has not altered over our time in Tuscany, although much else about wine moves on fast forward.

Changes continue to ring. In trattorias in the early nineties, you usually were asked, *"Nero o bianco?"* The waiter assumed that you would have Uncle Luca's or Armando's cousin's wine, black or white. We bought and enjoyed wine from a single shelf in the grocery store. Now Marco Molesini, whose family stills owns the grocery store, has become a sommelier. He runs a superbly curated shop of one thousand Italian wines right on Cortona's Piazza Repubblica. Arnaldo Rossi and Debora Zoccoloni's Taverna Pane e Vino, a wine bar/trattoria, adds further depth to the local scene, with their tastings and vintners' dinners. When we stop by, Arnaldo always has two bottles he wants to compare. On the steep streets leading into Cortona, several wine bars have opened. Even in the Coop supermarket down in the lower town, shelves are laden with the region's wine. Nearby Arezzo is experiencing a food renaissance, with numerous new wine establishments and restaurants. We're following a gold rush. Florence now has many atmospheric wine bars, such as Frescobaldi's on a tiny rabbit-leg street off the Piazza della Signoria, where you can have a light lunch with a lovely glass of their Brunello di Montalcino Castelgiocondo Riserva and still have the energy to seek out the Laurentian Library or the exhibit at the Strozzi.

In addition to innovative winemakers, I credit the Slow Food organization for this revolution. All over Italy, each chapter features tastings and food pairings. The local events are great fun, as well as educational. A dinner with food and wine from the Friuli or Piemonte with talks afterward by artisan cheesemakers, winemakers, and growers from the area definitely wakes up your interest. A focus on delicate Umbrian lentils or cave-aged cheeses or wild boar sausage or varieties of apples provides fascinating evenings. And we love meeting the winemakers. They're inevitably earthy and sophisticated, definitely ready for a good time. These events are occurring all over Italy, and, fortunately, are spreading in America. Vinitaly, an annual wine expo held every April, attracts wine lovers from all over the world, jamming Verona's fabled streets during the week of tastings, dinners, and parties.

Riccardo Bertocci worked at Avignonesi until he started his own wine consulting business. He knows more about Italian wine than anyone I've met, down to numbers of bottles, kind of corks, and histories of vineyards. And because of his weekly jaunts around Italy, he knows the best restaurants. Often, when we find ourselves somewhere without a plan—in Bologna, for example—we'll call Riccardo, who's usually at a wine-tasting in Bolzano or talking to a group of winemakers in Sicily. "Hey, we're in Bologna, where's the hot spot to eat?" Ed asks, and Riccardo will rattle off a half-dozen places and even remember if they're closed on Tuesdays. One July day last year in Arezzo, while we were at the monthly market, Ed called Riccardo to get a recommendation. He suggested the brand-new I Tre Bicchieri.

We told the owner, Stefano, that we were friends of Riccardo. We sat down, looked at their tome of a wine book, and Stefano, standing by quietly, smiled, "Would you like to try the best Sauvignon in Italy?" One can only answer yes to such a proposition, and we're glad we did, since Lafoa, a Sauvignon made by Colterenzio, in a flash became a favorite white, notwithstanding Stefano's praise: "It's enough just to smell it—smell the essence of *pipi di gatto,* the famous cat pee aroma." I never will understand wine lingo.

Two nights later, at Acquamatta in Capolona, we asked Paolo, the owner, for Lafoa. "We're out," he said. "But allow me to pour you something better." And so we discovered the pleasures of Sant Valentin, a most erudite white, soft and silky with a touch of flint. Lafoa and Sant Valentin, both from the northern Italian region, Alto Adige, which borders Austria and Switzerland, prove just how divine an Italian white can be.

These two Riccardos, Arnaldo, Marco, Stefano, and Paolo are all young men, passionately interested in wine. Their enthusiasm is infectious. Italy teems with this new energy.

❦

Bringing Tuscany home means enjoying wine with friends. It means rising to your feet to toast many of life's large and small celebrations. It means uncorking three bottles at once for the table, not the judicious opening of another only when one is finished.

Since we live half the year in California, we search the Bay Area for our particular preferences. We cellar a stash of Italian wines in California, which we've sent or hauled back. For special wines only, air freight from Italy is cost-effective. Even with the freight, the price is less than you would pay at a wine store. If you happen to be sending home a desk or chest, you can tuck in a couple of cases and the cost is negligible. The bonus is that you can take your memories home in a bottle. Many of Italy's one million vineyards are too small for export. The slip-of-a-white you drank on that jasmine-draped terrace overlooking the exact farm you'd like to own—it's not available *anywhere* in the States. It's easy to pack a box of wine carefully and check it with your luggage. The dollar or two per bottle duty, if collected, is negligible compared to wine prices in the United States. Anything I've lugged home, stuffed in the overhead compartment, or checked in a cheap duffel bought the day before departure, I've never regretted. It's especially festive on Thanksgiving or a birthday to offer a marvelous magnum of Avignonesi 50&50 or Poliziano Asinone, even if you have to hand-carry it.

When you're in Tuscany, try picking up the Italian way with wine. Engage the waiter. Order wine with lunch and dinner. Ask about the best local wines. Ask the waiter what he'd serve at his own wedding. I love the joy of no book, the joy of discovering on my own. Our Tuscan friends don't read wine guides. They go to the wine merchant, the waiter, the uncle, the vineyard down the road and talk, talk, talk. When in doubt, order the house wine. And a big bottle of water that you will promise to drink too. And if you've ordered house wine at lunch, you might try diluting it by the glass with the bottled water, as you'll see the *carabinieri* (state police) at the next table doing. This ancient Tuscan practice is called baptizing the wine. There will be no gasps of viticultural horror, although it's not to be recommended outside the trattoria lunch. While in Italy, pore over Gambero Rosso's *Italian Wines,* published annually in Italian and English, and then bring it home to use in your neighborhood wine store. If you're invited to dinner, take your hosts two or three bottles of wine, as the Italians do.

Ed and I often are off for weekends, with a delightfully empty trunk. I remember when we discovered the Morellino wines, a new word to us then. When I sip one of them now—and they're some of the jazziest Tuscan wines—I associate the taste with the Etruscan ruins that so enchanted us in the Scansano area. As you travel from place

WINE LIBRARY, IL FALCONIERE

to place, memories adhere to the wines. You'll taste the connection between the dark velvety Brunello and the purity of evensong at Sant' Antimo; between the structured Carmignano and the many-chimneyed Medici villa at Artimino; between the silvery, slippery white Vernaccia and the dawn light glancing off the Arno. This is wine's enchantment, a chanting meant for those lovers whose hearts are the color of wine.

At home again, you'll forget the one-hundred-degree heat and backing out of a one-way street. What occurred on the wine roads was, you'll realize, actually a great way to discover where a particular wine was really made, what wind was coursing around what mountain, what lettuces were on display at the weekly market, how the fennel tasted coming from a particular soil. In short, the splendor of *terroir,* all the natural factors that influence a grape to become one kind of wine rather than another. *Evviva la differenza!*

Often, we're so smitten by a bottle of great wine that we spend the day getting lost, trying to find the source of the pleasure, asking everyone for directions, getting various possibilities, then, finally, stumbling across an unlikely vineyard and ringing the doorbell. From a second-floor window, a woman leans out, about to shake a rug, and tells us, "Yes, we had wine, but it's all gone. You might try again next year." This isn't, we know, how it's done in California vineyards, with their parking lots and picnic tables, T-shirts, corkscrews, and etched wineglasses. Most of our travels are exhilarating—we arrive home dusty and tired, but often with a case or two of fabulous wine at fabulous prices, which we then share with our friends over a series of dinners inspired by new tastes.

The most meaningful aspect of opening a Tuscan wine at home is that a sun-drenched day returns in a rush, a day when you discovered an unassuming trattoria beside the road that is in no guide-book, where you loved every bite you took and every sip of the wine that had travelled only as far as from the tiny vineyard in the adjacent field to your table.

ETRUSCAN-STYLE PERGOLA
GRAPES IN CHIANTI

Toasts Among Friends

We asked four friends, all wine experts, to name their top choices for Super Tuscan, Chianti, Brunello di Montalcino, Vino Nobile di Montepulciano, and dessert wines. Not a "greatest hits" list, these are simply wines they love. Some of the choices overlap—especially wines from the Vino Nobile di Montepulciano area.

MARCO MOLESINI

Marco Molesini (pictured on page 188) owns the wine store Enoteca Molesini in Cortona. He has put together cases for many travelling friends of ours, who've been thrilled with his selections. Often, they reorder online.

SUPER TUSCAN

Oreno, Tenuta Sette Ponti

Cepparello, Isole e Olena

Grattamacco, Colle Massari

Ornellaia, Tenuta dell'Ornellaia

Masseto, Tenuta dell'Orenellaia

Romitorio di Santedame, Tenimenti Ruffino

Magari, Gaja

CHIANTI CLASSICO

Chianti Classico, Castello di Ama

Chianti Classico, San Giusto a Rentennano

Chianti Classico Vigna del Sorbo Riserva,
    Tenuta Fontodi

Fonterutoli, Castello di Fonterutoli

Berardenga, Fattoria di Felsina

BRUNELLO DI MONTALCINO

Tenuta Nuova, Casanova dei Neri

Castelgiocondo

La Casa, Tenuta Caparzo

Montosoli, Altesino

La Palazzetta

VINO NOBILE DI MONTEPULCIANO

Poliziano

Vigna Asinone, Poliziano

Grandi Annate, Avignonesi

Boscarelli

Vigneto Antica Chiusina, Fattoria del Cerro

DESSERT WINE

Passito di Pantelleria Ben Ryé, Tenuta di
    Donnafugata (Sicily)

Maximo, Umani Ronchi

Vin Santo, Avignonesi

ARNALDO ROSSI

Arnaldo Rossi raised the bar for wine service in Cortona when he and his wife opened Taverna Pane e Vino in arched rooms under a palazzo in Piazza Signorelli. Arnaldo chose wines that have *"un buon rapporto qualità-prezzo,"* a good connection between quality and price. He omitted Ornellaia, Masseto, Lupicaia, Vigna d'Alceo, Messorio, Vin Santo Avignonesi, and others, which, while being among Italy's best wines, are *carissimi,* very expensive, and are often difficult to find.

SUPER TUSCAN

Percarlo, San Giusto a Rentennano

Cortaccio, Villa Cafaggio

50&50, Avignonesi-Capannelle

Le Stanze, Poliziano

Cepparello, Isole e Olena

CHIANTI

Chianti Classico Riserva Casasilia, Poggio al Sole

Chianti Classico, Giorgio Primo, La Massa

Chianti Classico, Castello di Ama

Chianti Rufina Montesodi, Frescobaldi

Chianti Classico, Villa Cafaggio

BRUNELLO DI MONTALCINO

Uccelliera

Tenuta Oliveto

Tenutanuova, Casanova de Neri

Mastrojanni

La Fiorita

VINO NOBILE DI MONTEPULCIANO

Asinone, Poliziano

Grandi Annate, Avignonesi

Vigna del Nocio, Boscarelli

Salco, Salcheto

Poliziano

OTHER TUSCAN WINE OF NOTE

Carmignano, Villa di Capezzana, Tenuta di Capezzana

Cortona Il Bosco, Tenimenti Luigi D'Alessandro

Batar, Querciabella

Morellino di Scansano, Heba, Fattoria di Magliano

Con Vento, Tenuta del Terriccio

TOP VIN SANTO/DESSERT WINE

Vin Santo, Tenimenti Luigi D'Alessandro

Solalto, Le Pupille

Moscadello di Montalcino, La Poderina

RICCARDO BERTOCCI

Riccardo Bertocci was happy to give us his favorites, but cautioned, "There is no absolute favorite since the vintage, the food you are eating, the mood you are in, the people drinking with you are all decisive factors in establishing the chosen wine of the moment. The following are wines that during various times in my life (sometimes quite repeatedly) have given me superior emotions, glorious feelings, wines that have that extra something that make me thank God and Nature for allowing men and women to create such wonders."

SUPER TUSCAN

Oreno, Sette Ponti, for its elegance

Desiderio, Avignonesi, for the softness

San Martino, Villa Cafaggio, for its true Tuscan nature

Percarlo, San Giusto a Rentennano, for the emotion

Fontalloro, Felsina, for the tradition

Ardito, Riccardo Baracchi, for the mixture of land and love

Do Ut Des, Carpineta Fontalpino, for the sensuality only
   a woman winemaker can give to her wine

CHIANTI

Chianti Classico, Villa Cafaggio, for the true taste of
   Sangiovese

Chianti Classico Riserva Cellole, San Fabiano Calcinaia,
   for the power

Chianti Classico Riserva Rancia, Felsina, for the
   first time

Chianti Classico Riserva Capraia, di Rocca di Castagnoli,
   for the memories

BRUNELLO DI MONTALCINO

Tenuta Nuova, Casanova di Neri, for the taste of
   the land
Vigna del Lago, Val di Suga, for the memories again
Poggio di Sotto, for the subtlety
Casanuova delle Cerbaie, for the surprise

VINO NOBILE DI MONTEPULCIANO

Vigna del Nocio, Boscarelli, for the love of earth
Riserva Grandi Annate, Avignonesi, for the aroma
Vigna dell'Asinone, Poliziano, for the power

OTHER TUSCAN WINE OF NOTE

Rosso di Avignonesi, for the best value
Belcore, Giusti e Zanza, for the difference
Cortona Il Bosco, Tenimenti Luigi
   D'Alessandro, for the first love
Rosso di Montalcino Banditella, Col d'Orcia,
   for its drinkability
Rosso di Montepulciano, Villa Sant'Anna,
   for its feminine virtues
Vernaccia di San Gimignano Vigna Santa Chiara,
Palagetto, for the persuasion of its taste

The top *vin santo* is by far the Vin Santo, Avignonesi (with their Occhio di Pernice a close second), but its rarity and price make it a very difficult, although unforgettable, experience. Remember that true *vin santo* can only be made in small quantities and the price has to be high. Three other more manageable *vin santi* of genuine and high quality are:

Vin Santo Toscano, San Giusto a Rentennano
Vin Santo, Castello di Cacchiano
Vin Santo, Selvapiana

I FRATELLI WINE BAR IN FLORENCE

Silvia Regi of Il Falconiere found it very difficult to choose because "There are so many good wines now in Tuscany." She and Riccardo produce the Ardito and Smeriglio that we would put on any list.

SUPER TUSCAN

Dulcamara, I Giusti e Zanza

Cerviolo, San Fabiano in Calcinaia

Livernano, Livernano

Avvoltore, Moris Farms

Do Ut Des, Carpineta Fontalpino

Campaccio, Fattoria di Terrabianca

Corbaia, Castello di Bossi

Gualdo del Re, Gualdo del Re

CHIANTI

Chianti Classico Cellole Riserva, San Fabiano in
   Calcinaia

Chianti Classico Berardo Riserva, Castello di Bossi

Chianti Classico Poggio al Sole, Casasilia

Chianti Rufina Bucerchiale, Selvapiana

Chianti Classico, Villa Cafaggio

BRUNELLO DI MONTALCINO

Siro Pacenti

Fanti, Tenuta San Filippo

Poggio di Sotto

Agostina Pieri

Talenti

VINO NOBILE DI MONTEPULCIANO

Avignonesi

Vigna del Nocio, Boscarelli

Vigna dell'Asinone, Poliziano

Canneto

Tenuta Val di Piatta

VIN SANTO

Vin Santo, Fabbri

WINES CURRENTLY POURED AT OUR HOUSE

WINES THAT PROMOTE GREAT CONVERSATION

Ardito, Baracchi

Vino Nobile di Montepulciano, Vigna del Nocio,
   Boscarelli

Gabbiano Bellezza and Gabbiano Alleanza

MEDITATIVE WINES

Sagrantino di Montefalco, Caprai (Umbria)

Brunello di Montalcino, Tenimenti Angelini, Val di Suga

WINES FOR ROMANCE

Brunello di Montalcino, Poggio Antico

Saffredi, Le Pupille

Fontalloro, Fattori di Felsina

WINES TO SHARE WITH A CLOSE FRIEND

Avvoltore, Moris Farms

Desiderio, Avignonesi

WINES FOR A WEDNESDAY-NIGHT DINNER

Fonte al Sole, Ruffino

Col di Sasso, Banfi

Cortona Fontarca, Tenimenti Luigi D'Alessandro

Rosso di Montepulciano, Avignonesi

WINES FOR THE GREAT OCCASION

Brunello di Montalcino, La Casa, Caparzo

Siepi, Castello di Fonterutoli

Oreno, Tenuta Sette Ponti

BRINGING TUSCANY HOME

"Signora Mayes, I would like to make a comment," a man called out from the back of the audience. I had just finished a talk at the Chicago library and had opened the floor for questions. "You describe a beautiful Tuscany," he said, "a Tuscany I know well. I was born in and grew up in Arezzo. But here tonight I would like to tell you something." He paused. "I am in Chicago for the same reasons you are in Tuscany. Tuscany, Signora, is a state of mind." We all laughed and then I agreed.

Tuscany as a state of mind makes sense to a southerner who was spoon-fed the sense of place, along with cheese grits and smothered quail. I've always found that people respond to place in a deeply idiosyncratic way. The place you recognize as yours, only yours, is a lucky connection. Even now, I'm always looking for it when I travel. *Could I live here? What's it like to wake up facing this shore? Would I ever tire of the big, smeary sunsets? How many ways are there to cook blue crab? Will the waves enter my dreams?* The place you choose *will* form you and will make you what you are to become.

On the first day I spent in a rented house in Tuscany in 1985, I dug holes with a kitchen spoon and put six basil plants in the ground. After a dinner of pasta with fresh tomatoes, we sat outside on the terrace. I could see a crumbled farm in the moonlight across a field. The next day I walked over and began to calculate the square footage of the pigpen and to look at where the morning sun struck the missing windows. *Sell everything—it's worth the risk,* I thought. It was five more years before I actually bought Bramasole, but by the end of the idyllic month in the country, my basil had proliferated and my passion for a way of life was flourishing even more wildly.

What caught me so surely? I've often wondered. What gives that ready identification with a place that's so much like falling in love? I already knew I loved the piazzas, the vibrant Italian life, the art, and the painterly landscape. When I place myself back there, I come again and again to the timelessness of the Tuscan house. Inside it, I felt fresh rushes of happiness. I felt as though I were held in a large hand. The naturalness of stone, the open, arched doors, and the silence I floated in during the nights gave me a new sensation. As if I were home, really home. How strange to experience that in a country not your own. Like a small boat raised and lowered by the tides, I was buoyed and rocked by the rhythms of deep-country life. Time—to be at home in time is a great gift. This is the first cornerstone of what a Tuscan home is about—the ease of days, the measure of hours exceeding the day's requirements, the seasons working their spells, and always the great Mediterranean sun warming your bones.

Finding *home* after that July became a quest, which culminated when I found Bramasole and began a new writing life on that hillside under the Etruscan wall. This is my fourth book springing spontaneously from the intense *gioia di vivere,* joy of living, among Tuscans. For Ed and me, creating our homes and gardens, spending mornings in the kitchen, gathering friends to our table, anchors our days. Though the philosophers don't write extensively about the concept of home, or even the

pursuit of happiness, they do write about beauty, that second cornerstone of Tuscan life. Actually making beauty around you honors all of life.

One of my pleasures has been that family, friends, and strangers have felt the same response to this place that I did. For many years a mysterious man left flowers in the shrine at the bottom of our driveway every day. When he disappeared, other people began to come to the house, often leaving coins, letters, pinecones, feathers—little symbols under the ceramic Mary. Last summer, I found a note:

> Dear Frances,
> *Bramasole.* No longer a simple name or a name with a history, but a philosophy and a way of life. To breathe the summer sun's heat, to walk calmly through the pristine green of the cypress and wild flowers' volatile parfums, to listen to the holy chants of nature's choir is to live as a Bramasolist. Bramasole—a subtle, passive verb: *to bramasole.*
> . . . We leave you this note and a bouquet of wild flowers as a metaphorical thanks (bramasolist simplicity) for what you have brought to two 21- and 24-year-old lovers.

I've kept the note on my desk, charmed by the invention. For my Tuscan friend in Chicago, I've imagined his excitement over the architecture along the lake, his bramasolist Saturday mornings at the Art Institute, his kitchen where a huge American breakfast is on the table, his evenings in the dense blue light of jazz clubs. I'm happy that he has brought Tuscany home.

UNA PICCOLA GUIDA
A LITTLE GUIDE

That most glorious inheritance of the Renaissance, the artisan tradition, thrives in Tuscany. I must have peered into a thousand minute workshops where someone was hand-gilding a frame, carving a finial, restoring a worn patch on a canvas, blowing glass, painting a plate, or drawing a complex marquetry design. In every town, take the narrow street, then one even narrower. In these old neighborhoods, a man refinishes a table out on the sidewalk. Four young women remove cups from a kiln. A very intense young man paints a toy horse. Respond to the written invitation to ring the bell. Inside, you're catapulted into the atmosphere of medieval guilds. Discovering special objects for your home becomes part of the meaning and fun of travel, especially in Tuscany, because the tradition of *a mano,* by hand, links to the deepest values of the culture.

Souvenir means to come to the aid of memory. Despite the connection with tawdry tchotchke shops, I've always liked the word. Pilgrims always have returned home with something in hand. Whether you bring back a quartz rock picked up on the path leading to an Etruscan tomb or a seventeenth-century still life of lemons, at a glance, the souvenir takes you back. As in an intimate journal or an album of photographs, memory resides in that particular treasure that says *I was there.* This is one of the affirming joys of travel.

This chapter consists of my highly personal recommendations. I wish I were organized enough to have a neat little black book, but, instead, I've compiled this chapter from dozens of business cards, menus, notes scrawled on maps and scraps of paper at the bottoms of my handbags. What follows is only a *for instance.* Meandering in intriguing towns, you will find the lively artisan tradition all over Tuscany.

Since you will find the famous shops such as Frette, Pratesi, Richard Ginori, Pinader, etc. on your own, my suggestions for exploring the artisan tradition veer more toward the nooks and byways, the weekly outdoor markets in every Tuscan town, and the places where the local people shop. There you discover the objects that only *you* could select. That is what ultimately makes your home original.

The most ordinary stores in any Tuscan town attract both of us. *Tabacchi* (tobacco) stores, now that people smoke less, often carry beautiful calendars, fountain pens, and stationery. Ivan's Tabaccheria del Corso in Cortona has expanded to include a gallery, Il Pozzo, for photography exhibits and handmade paper. Garden centers sell seeds for all the Tuscan lettuces you'll see at the *frutta e verdura,* as well as several basils.

We especially like hardware stores. Usually they stock an extensive selection of knobs, drawer pulls, handles, and keys. You could fool me—they look old. I found unusual bronze pulls for all my kitchen drawers for a fraction of what they would cost at home. And, of course, they were unique. Hardware stores stock *fustini,* stainless-steel kegs for olive oil, with little faucets for filling a bottle. They come in all sizes and the smallest ones are perfect for a pantry shelf. Ed is always on the lookout for espresso pots. Besides the Mokas in all sizes, you may come upon charming two-cup stovetop pots in stainless steel or Alessi designs. Often, too, you can find handwoven olive-picking baskets, made to strap around your waist. They're handy for picking fruit at home or for holding mail on your desk. They sell the handy grills Tuscans use in their fireplaces at home, hunting knives, grape-trimming knives, copper pots, andirons, and sometimes the baskets and ironwork of local craftspeople. The people who run hardware stores know their business. During the restoration of Bramasole, they helped educate us. Around Cortona, they still joke to us, "Too bad for us you finished your house."

It's fun to look in *bomboniere*, confection shops, for celebration favors. If you have a few days, they can personalize communion, birthday, or wedding mementos, or print small cards with the honoree's name. Usually these shops are ablaze with kitsch but also have tasteful place cards and small favors for important occasions. That so many of them exist attests to the frequency of celebration in Tuscan life.

Paper stores are everywhere. I go in every one I see, always in search of perfect materials that will make writing a breeze. The well-known Il Papiro chain has long been a favorite. I have visiting cards printed at their shop in Cortona. They have whimsical designs, not at all formal. Il Papiro is also centrally located in Siena, with several shops in Florence. One is near the Duomo at Piazza Duomo, 24r. Carteria Tassotti, another tempting shop in Florence, is also near the Duomo: via dei Servi 9 / 11 r. From there, I bring home art tubes of thick wrapping papers for lining drawers in patterns of watermelons, books, architectural designs, cherries, etc. My shelf for gifts is stocked with paper-covered boxes and folio covers. Smaller artisan shops are not hard to find for leather- or vellum-bound blank books, hand-marbled papers, memorable photograph albums, desk pads, and stationery. Many of the artisan shops, such as Stefano Villani's Il Parione (via Parione, 10r in Florence) will have those oversized visiting cards that look so distinctive. If you're not staying long enough, the shop will mail them home to you. At Stefano's the integrity of the artistry is such that you can return a photo album for repair after ten years if the binding comes loose.

Almost every town has an art gallery, where the most exciting discoveries can happen. Amid generic fluff produced for mass tourism, genuine quality paintings can be found and easily brought or sent home. Since art is always the revealing news of a culture, a watercolor or drawing you love will give you pleasure all your life.

The monthly antique market, *la fiera,* in Arezzo has furnished many corners of Bramasole, Fonte delle Foglie, and my house in California, as well as inspired pieces for my furniture collection with Drexel Heritage. Every first weekend of the month, all year, the Piazza Grande and surrounding streets turn into a vast medieval market. The September market is the largest—you'll need both Saturday and Sunday for that one. At the fair you'll find antiques that you had no idea you could buy—whole altars, medieval wells, immense iron gates. My quests are usually for more portable objects. I look for vintage linens and fabrics, garden antiques, framed prints, paintings, plate racks, leather books, chandeliers, reliquaries, iron crosses, sconces, hand-painted tiles, candlesticks, *armadi,* and objects I did not know I wanted: crocks, wine harvest baskets, deco sugar and flour canisters, an old violin, or the carved foot of a saint. Do not expect to find silver or fine china. Two friends who collect medieval ceramics often find pieces at the market. I always look for the rough guys from Naples. Who knows where they find their wares? From them, I bought fanciful garden urns with putti on the sides. Steven discovered a marble holy water font carved in the shape of a shell, which serves as a secular art object. At the market, ask the price. You're then expected to suggest a lower one. Usually the dealer will meet you in the middle. You'll almost always get at least 10 to 20 percent off. Nothing in Tuscany compares to the Arezzo market. Even nonshoppers will be entranced by the colorful variety of goods and people.

On any day, you can browse in dozens of antique shops on Arezzo's upper Corso Italia and the streets radiating from the Piazza Grande. I especially admire Galleria Etruria on the Corso at #12. Guidieri Pasqualino keeps to the highest standards. I found my blue-gray bookcase at his booth at an antique fair and he shipped it home for me. Arezzo's fare includes astounding fourteenth-century painted wood angels, medieval benches, marquetry chests, credenzas, and iron beds. The shops take credit cards but will give you a better price if you pay cash.

Other regular antique fairs in Tuscany take place in Lucca (Piazza Antelminelli) on the third weekend of every month, Siena (Loggiati di San Domenico) on the third Sunday, and

Carmignano (Piazza Vittorio Emmanuele) on the first Sunday. You'd think Florence would have a great market but we must be content with the hundreds of *favolosi* antique shops in the twisting backstreets. Cruise Via Maggio and the entire Oltrarno. I've never found anything at the various periodic or ongoing markets, but friends have spotted a few treasures. A refined national antique market, Mostra Mercato Nazionale di Mobile Antico (Palazzo Vagnotti) takes place in Cortona every year in the last week of August and the first week of September. Bagarre, the annual Parma antique market (in Emilia Romagna) held at the fairgrounds is legendary. Check the website for the date each year: www.fiere.parma.it.

ANTIQUES

ANTICHITÀ ROBERTO AND UMBERTO BIANCHI
VIA GIOTTO, 77 ✣ LE VILLE, MONTERCHI
TEL.: 0575 709026
Roberto and his father specialize in garden antiques and fireplaces. I found a nineteenth-century gazebo and the eighteenth-century fireplace for the mountain house there. They also have marble sinks, paintings, signs, and antique iron objects. Le Ville is near those Piero della Francesca meccas, Monterchi and Sansepolcro.

ARTE ANTICA
VIA G. MATTEOTTI, 132 ✣ CAMUCIA, NEAR CORTONA
TEL.: 338 9340 758
Small showroom and large warehouse.
Call for appointment

BEATO ANGELICO
PIAZZA SIGNORELLI, 4, AND A LARGER SHOP
RIGHT DOWN VIA NAZIONALE ✣ CORTONA
TEL.: 0575 603782
Isa Miretta knows the provenance of everything in her shops. Through her, shipping is a breeze. Her daughter restores historic painted fans and they have a collection in the shops, which are otherwise focused on Tuscan furniture.

BRUNO BERTOCCI
VIA DEL MORO, 3 ✣ CAMUCIA, NEAR CORTONA
TEL.: 0575 603399
Bruno helped me make beds and bookcases. In his large shop and warehouse, I've found an eighteenth-century painted chest and an *armadio*. He's an excellent resource because of his wide connections around Tuscany.

FURNITURE

MAURIZIO PONZIANI
VIA SANTO SPIRITO, 27 ✻ FLORENCE
TEL.: 055 287958
High-quality painted reproduction furniture. Custom shop with large archive to peruse. They produce whatever you want. We lived down the street from this shop one summer and never could resist a stop.

DREXEL HERITAGE
1925 EASTCHESTER DRIVE
HIGH POINT, NORTH CAROLINA 27265
TEL.: 866-450-3434
WWW.DREXELHERITAGE.COM
My contribution to bringing Tuscany home is the "At Home in Tuscany Collection," available at Drexel Heritage stores. The beds, chests, *armadi,* chairs, tables, upholstered furniture, bookcases, and other pieces in the collection were designed from our antiques at Bramasole, furniture we shipped home, and from inspirations gathered when we travelled around Tuscany with the DH design team. Fabrics reflect fresco colors. The collection also has the following extensions:

LANEVENTURE outdoor furniture, www.laneventure.com

SFERRA BROS. LTD. luxurious Tuscan bed and table linens, www.sferrabros.com and info@sferrabros. com

WILDWOOD LAMPS lamps inspired by wooden candlesticks, the *ferro battuto* craft of ironwork, and Tuscan urns, www.wildwoodlamps.com and www.russatwildwoodlamps.com

VIETRI Bramasole dinnerware and pewter cutlery, www.vietri.com

MIRESCO RUGS striped and monochromatic handwoven rugs, www.miresco.com

STONE AND MARBLE

ARTE DECORATIVA DI SIMONE FIORDELISI
VIA DE' BARBADORI, 41R ✻ FLORENCE
TEL.: 055 215766
WWW.FIRENZE-OLTRARNO.NET
Handmade tables and chessboards. The Medicis were fond of marble inlaid with designs in colored stones, a craft called *pietra dura,* hard stone. At this artisan shop, they display tables with traditional bird and flower designs from Pompeii in many sizes, as well as geometric designs.

RAFFAELLO ROMANELLI
LUNGARNO ACCIAIOLI 72-78R ✻ FLORENCE
TEL.: 055 2396662
WWW.ARCA.NET/MALL/ROMANELLI
Paperweights, bookends, rulers made with twelve colors of marble, spheres, obelisks, inlaid marble boxes, plus large garden figures.

SCAGLIOLA

BIANCO BIANCHI E FIGLI
VIALE EUROPA, 117 (SECOND FLOOR)
FLORENCE
TEL.: 055 686118
Scagliola, scales, is an ancient art form. Shards of a form of gypsum are ground, colored with natural pigments, bound with animal mordant, then applied into designs incised into marble or stone. The borders, frames, panels, and tables are then sealed and waxed. A fascinating craft. The workshop in Pontassieve also can be visited by appointment. If you're interested in *pietra dura* and *scagliola,* visit the Museo dell'Opificio delle Pietre Dure in Florence.

ALABASTER

Alabaster has the lovely quality of transparency. This Etruscan town is the center for alabaster works, from simple vases and cups, to pellucid bowls and sconces. Volterra is a mysterious town with an excellent museum of paintings and a tradition of good food. Wander in and out of the twenty-five small bottegas around the town, which actively keep this tradition alive.

COOPERATIVA ARTIERI
PIAZZA DEI PRIORI, 5 ✻ VOLTERRA
TEL.: 0588 87590

ROSSI ALABASTRI
VIA LUNGO LE MURA DEL MANDORLO, 7 ✻ VOLTERRA
TEL.: 0588 86133

TERRA-COTTA

POGGI UGO
VIA IMPRUNETANA PER TAVARNUZZE, 16
IMPRUNETA
TEL.: 055 2011077
WWW.POGGIUGO.IT

M.I.T.A.L. (MANIFATTURA IMPRUNETANA TERRECOTTE
ARTISTICHE E LATERIZI)
VIA DI CAPPELLO, 31 ✣ IMPRUNETA
TEL.: 055 2011414
WWW.MITAL.RTD.IT

Traditional terra-cotta in the ancient center of this craft.
Busts, floor tiles, wall sconces, garden plaques, olive oil
jars, amphoras, fruit baskets, wine coolers, plus the classic
pots for lemons. These are two of the major stops for
terra-cotta but Impruneta is a maze of terra-cotta artisans.

CERAMICS

MAIOLICHE OTELLO DOLFI
VIA TOSCO ROMAGNOLA, 8/6
CAMAIONI, JUST OUTSIDE MONTELUPO
TEL.: 0571 910105
WWW.OTELLODOLFI.IT

Montelupo is only eight miles from Florence. The only
game in town is ceramics. Before you go, print out the list
of members of the Association of Ceramics Artisans in
Montelupo found at www.leonet.it/firms. Some of the artisans are located in nearby Montespertoli and Camaioni. For
the historical context of the local art, tour the Museo
Archeologico e della Ceramica di Montelupo, via
Bartolomeo Sinibaldi, 43, and visit their website at
www.museomontelupo.it.

UBALDO GRAZIA
VIA TIBERINA, 181 ✣ DERUTA
TEL.: 075 9710201
WWW.UBALDOGRAZIA.COM

The entire Umbrian town of Deruta is devoted to hand-
painted majolica. Wander around the town center then
drive out along the via Tiberina, where you will find dozens
of shops. A stop at Ubaldo Grazia is obligatory. Ring the
bell and bypass the first room. In the back, they stock a
great variety of traditional patterns. Some may be pur-
chased on the spot; others must be ordered and the wait is
long. You can arrange for your own design to be made, or
customize one of theirs with the name of your house or
your monogram.

CERAMICHE UMBRE
TIRIDUZZI BRUNO & C.
VIA D. ZIPIROVIC
SASSO, JUST A LOOP UNDER THE FREEWAY
FROM VIA TIBERINA IN DERUTA
TEL.: 075 972178
WWW.TIRIDUZZI.IT

Glazed, hand-painted tables made from fired volcanic
stone called *peperino*, for its black flecks. Although the tables look like ceramic, they are durable outdoors. The
lemon patterns are cheerful and appealing. A white blue-
bordered round table with lemons and foliage could move
right into a garden room. The staff will work with you on
your own design as well.

PRINTS AND FRAMES

In the Oltrarno neighborhood, just over the Ponte
Vecchio in Florence, many craftsmen practice their arts.
The warren of small streets is heaven for Oriental rugs,
antiques, and intimate print shops. I like to spend a morning looking at maps, architectural drawings, botanicals,
fauna, landscapes. Unframed prints are easy to bring home
because they can be layered in the suitcase, but the intaglio
and painted frames are so exquisite, it's tempting to let the
shop frame your choice and mail it to you, or to buy a
frame for a mirror.

BOTTEGA DELLE STAMPE
BORGO SAN JACOPO, 56R ✣ FLORENCE
TEL.: 055 295396

AQUA FORTIS
ADC DI PIERLIUGI FRANCHI & C. S.A.S.
BORGO SAN JACOPO, 80/R ✣ FLORENCE
TEL.: 055 292164
WWW.AQUAFORTIS.CO

F.LLI SARTIE C.
BORGO SAN JACOPO, 40R ✣ FLORENCE
TEL.: 055 2381386

CAFISSI
VIA LAVORNO, 8/5 ✣ FLORENCE
TEL.: 055 7327273
WWW.CAFISSI.COM

Tastefully painted wooden trays and wastebaskets.

MOSCARDI FRAME SHOP ON THE ARNO, FLORENCE

BRINGING TUSCANY HOME

C. MOSCARDI
LUNGARNO CORSINI, 36R ✤ FLORENCE
TEL.: 055 214414
The ultimate frame shop.

MIRRORS

VETRERIA ARTISTICA DI R.E M. SCHIAVON
FONDAMENTA VETRAI, 7 ✤ MURANO
TEL.: 041 739396

DETAIL OF THE VENETIAN MIRROR

TEXTILES

BUSATTI LINENS
VIA MAZZINI, 14 ✤ ANGHIARI, NEAR SANSEPOLCRO
TEL.: 0575 788013
WWW.BUSATTI.COM
Busatti's factory is located just off the long street Ritta,
where since 1338 a market has been held in the piazza,
now under the watchful gaze of Garibaldi. You can buy
fabric by the meter or order duvet covers, table linens,
curtains, and cushions made to measure. Shops also in
Città di Castello and Arezzo.

PASSAMANERIA TOSCANA
PIAZZA SAN LORENZO, 12R ✤ FLORENCE
TEL.: 055 2381666

Just behind the San Lorenzo market, the place for pillows,
runners, fringes, tassels, and trims, plus a small selection
of luxurious silk fabrics.

VALMAR LA PASSAMANERIA
VIA PORTA ROSSA, 53R ✤ FLORENCE
TEL.: 055 284493
WWW.VALMAR-FLORENCE.COM
Similar to above.

ANTICO SETIFICIO FIORENTINO
VIA L. BARTOLINI, 4 ✤ FLORENCE
TEL.: 055 213 861
Fabulous handwoven silks and damasks, also small articles
such as evening bags, potpourri bags, jewelry rolls, and
scarves.

LISIO TESSUTI D'ARTE
VIA DEI FOSSI, 45R ✤ FLORENCE
TEL.: 055 212430
Handwoven fabric in designs taken from historic and
artistic patterns.

LORENZO RUBELLI
VIA DEI FOSSI, 37-39R ✤ FLORENCE
TEL.: 055 2608605
Fabrics for the home, some inspired by historic patterns.

LORETTA CAPONI
PIAZZA ANTINORI, 4R ✤ FLORENCE
TEL.: 055 213668
Fine table and bed linens in a luxurious shop, also fairy
princess smocked dresses for children and exquisite at-
home loungewear.

TESSUTO ARTISTICO UMBRO
PIAZZA DEL COMUNE ✤ MONTEFALCO
One of the most characteristic Umbrian towns is home to
a weaving tradition. The cotton and linen fabrics are similar in quality to Tuscan ones, but with different designs
and colors. Montefalco is also the home of one of Ed's
A-list wines, Sagrantino di Montefalco.

STENCILS

THE STENCIL LIBRARY
TEL: 011 441 661 844 844
WWW.STENCIL-LIBRARY.COM
Located in Northumberland, this archive of more than
3,500 stencils can be browsed online. The owners ship
worldwide.

Romanesque fountains, dining room tables, historic fans, bookcases—anything can be shipped. Antique dealers are well connected with local expediters and will be able to handle your shipment. They'll have your special chair or bench enclosed in a sturdy wooden crate and fully insure it. Although air is not always prohibitively expensive, generally the most economical route is by sea. By air, your shipment will arrive in three to five days. By sea, it can be six to eight weeks. You also can ask at your hotel or check the local tourist office for shippers in a given area. In Florence, a shipping office on Via della Scala off Piazza Santa Maria Novella, across from the Farmacia Santa Maria Novella, will handle your large and small purchases.

CHANDELIERS & SCONCES

ENNE TI
BORGO SAN FREDIANO, 44R ✵ FLORENCE
TEL.: 055 284257

CUTLERY

CONAZ COLTELLERIE
VIA G. GIORDANI, 20 ✵ SCARPERIA
TEL.: 055 846197
WWW.CONAZ.COM
Scarperia, in the Mugello above Florence, has a long history of making knives. Some gourmets carry their own Scarperia knives with them to restaurants. Of sculptural design purity, these finely honed knives flick off a wine foil or slice into a *bistecca*. A knife market of *ferri taglienti*, cutting iron, is held each year, August 30–September 14, at the Palazzo dei Vicari. Look into the Fratelli Consigli's store for knives with handles of bull horn, shell, and rosewood with over four hundred kinds of blades. The town has a museum chronicling the history of the craft: Museo dei Ferri Taglienti at Palazzo dei Vacari.

ARTISAN CRAFTS

EMPORIO TOSCANO
VIA FONTEBRANDA, 65 ✵ SIENA
TEL.: 0577 226305
A gathering of artisan products for the home. One-of-a-kind ceramics, iron objects, marble carvings, and textiles.

SILVER

GUIDO SISTI
PIAZZA DELLA VITTORIA, 16
CAPOLONA, NEAR AREZZO
TEL.: 0575 421074
WWW.GUIDOSISTI.IT
Handmade silver serving pieces. Instant heirlooms.

CRYSTAL

MOLERIA LOCCHI
VIA BURCHIELLO, 10 ✵ FLORENCE
TEL.: 055 2298371
Near Porta Romana, this very particular shop makes crystal glasses, decanters, or whatever you want. They repair treasures with snapped stems, or copy the delicate wineglass that shattered in the sink.

SANTA MARIA NOVELLA PHARMACY
VIA DELLA SCALA, 16N ✣ FLORENCE
TEL.: 055 216276
WWW.SMNOVELLA.IT

After visiting the frescoes of Ghirlandaio and Masaccio in Santa Maria Novella, cross the piazza and turn down the narrow street, via della Scala, where you enter the church's Officina Profumo Farmaceutica. People who feared plague and pox sought out cures, tinctures, and herbal preparations here. An atmosphere of sanctity remains in this polar opposite of Walgreens. The pharmacy still concocts "alimentary integrators" made with bladder wrack, dog rose, willow, and devil's claw. I love their burning papers (room fragrance), toothpastes, pure soaps, and wax tablets to scent a room. Their intense, spicy potpourri you'll love or hate. I use it in my pantry. Steven brings me their terra-cotta pomegranates infused with scent to hang in closets.

UN ASSAGIO DI TOSCANA

A TASTE OF TUSCANY

The enormous popularity of Italian food in America makes finding *farro,* semolina flour, salted capers, and a hundred other items much easier than even a few years ago. The best news of all is the expansion and flowering of farmers' markets and the new awareness of superior local produce. The good purveyors, Dean & DeLuca and Williams-Sonoma, sell a plethora of goodies for *la cucina.* A little Internet research will turn up any Italian cheese you want and any balsamic vinegar. I recommend A.G. Ferrari on the West Coast and A Southern Season in Chapel Hill, N.C. While travelling in Italy, stop in at *alimentari,* small grocery stores, whose crowded shelves yield many easy treats, some of which I mention in the chapter *Butta la Pasta!* They will also prepare your hunk of *parmigiano* or pecorino *sotto vuoto,* shrink wrapped, so that you can transport it easily.

Both in Italy and the United States, the Slow Food organization offers exceptional activities. See their website, www.slowfood.com, for information on Vinitaly, the annual wine expo in Verona, the Cheese expo in Bra, and the Tasting Salon in Turin. For information on local chapters and activities, see www.slowfoodusa.org.

OLIVE OIL

OLIO & CONVIVIUM
VIA S. SPIRITO, 4 ✤ FLORENCE
TEL.: 055 2658198
A fine range of Tuscan olive oils, as well as other local products, and a perfect place for lunch.

BRAMASOLE OLIVE OIL
TEL.: 1 877 TOSCANA
WWW.THETUSCANSUN.COM
Pure, unfiltered extra virgin olive oil from our region, imported by my daughter, Ashley, and her friend Nico Peruzzi. Our handpicked olives are blended with those of other local growers. Acid level is .1 percent, well below the 1 percent amount that qualifies oil as extra virgin. The lower the acid, the better the oil. A portion of the profit, if there ever is any, will be donated to the City of Cortona for various improvement projects.

CASTELLO DI FONTERUTOLI
EXTRA-VIRGIN OLIVE OIL
WWW.FONTERUTOLI.IT
The great winemakers also produce this extra virgin olive oil from olives picked early. A spicy, fragrant oil.

ACADEMIA BARILLA
WWW.ACADEMIABARILLA.COM
The Academia bottles seven regional extra virgin oils from different parts of Italy. One is from Chianti. Available in specialty stores.

WINE

We recommend the readable *Vino Italiano* by David Lynch and Joseph Bastianich for its excellent and up-to-date survey of regional wines, as well as *Best Wines of Italy* by Burton Anderson. Gambero Rosso, www.gamberorosso.com publishes the essential yearly guide, *Italian Wines.*

ENOTECA ITALIANA
MEDICI FORTRESS ✤ SIENA
WWW.ENOTECA-ITALIANA.IT
This unique national *enoteca* offers cool respite from hot streets. All the regions of Italy are represented by their best wines. Taste by the glass, buy what you like, and tour the collection with a sommelier.

ENOTECA MOLESINI
PIAZZA DELLA REPUBBLICA ✤ 52044 CORTONA (AR)
TEL.: 0575 60432
WWW.WINESHIP@MOLESINI-MARKET.COM

TAVERNA PANE E VINO
PIAZZA SIGNORELLI, 27 ✤ 52044 CORTONA (AR)
TEL.: 0575 631010
WWW.PANE-VINO.IT
Arnaldo and Debora also operate a very mellow trattoria.

VINITALY
WWW.VINITALYONLINE.COM
The huge wine exhibition in Verona each spring. Through its listings, you'll be able to gather websites of a number of Italian wineries.

ITALIAN TRADE COMMISSION
WWW.ITALIANMADE.COM
This "Official Site of the Foods and Wines of Italy" is a great source for information not just on DOC, DOCG, and IGP areas in Italy, but also about the regions of Italy, their foods and recipes.

Because of the thousands and thousands of Italian wines, American importers and wine shops can only stock a fraction. Happily, that fraction can be quite good to extraordinary. Still, if you are an aficionado of Italian wines, most American shops will seem quite disappointedly limited. If you find a good local retailer and establish a friendship, chances are they'll be able to find the wines you want from various distributors. If your local wine shop fails you, there are excellent online retailers.

ITALIAN WINE MERCHANT
108 EAST 16TH STREET ✤ NEW YORK, NY 10003
TEL.: 212 473 2323
WWW.ITALIANWINEMERCHANT.COM

VINO, ITALIAN WINE AND SPIRITS
121 EAST 27TH STREET ✤ NEW YORK, NY 10016
TEL.: 212 725 6516
WWW.VINOSITE.COM

ZACHY'S
16 EAST PARKWAY ✤ SCARSDALE, NY 10583
TEL.: 800 723 0241
WWW.ZACHYS.COM

WINE BARS IN FLORENCE

Florence always has had wine cantinas for a quick glass with friends, but recently this tradition has virtually exploded. And now, you'll find a wine bar on the main street of many hill towns. Florence's new wine bars offer a convivial introduction to the range of Tuscan wines.

CAFFÈ ITALIANO
VIA DELLA CONDOTTA, 56R

CANTINE DEI VERRAZZANO
VIA DEI TAVOLINI, 18/20R
TEL.: 055 268590

CASA DEL VINO
VIA DELL'ARIENTO, 16R

ENOTECA FUORI PORTA
VIA DEL MONTE ALLE CROCI
FLORENCE
TEL.: 055 2342483
Terrific wine list to sample and wines to go as well.

FRESCOBALDI
VIA DE' MAGAZZINI, 2-4R
The walls are as delightful as the wines.

GUSTAVINO
VIA DELLA CONDOTTA, 37R

I FRATELLINI
VIA DEI CIMATORI, 38R
Nontrendy, tiny, on-the-street wine bar, pouring for Florentines since 1875.

IL VINAIO
PIAZZA DEL GRANO, 10
A wine shop where you also can sample sausages and that Tuscan specialty, *lampredotto*—don't ask, don't tell.

LE VOLPI E L'UVA
PIAZZA DEI ROSSI, 1R

VINI E VECCHIE SAPORI
VIA DE' MAGAZZINI, 3R

IN GIRO
TRAVELLING

HOTELS, RESIDENCES, AND RESTAURANTS

The following are mentioned in the text, with a few other recommendations.

TORNABUONI BEACCI HOTELS
VIA DE' TORNABUONI, 3 ⁕ FLORENCE
TEL.: 055 212645
WWW.TORNABUONIHOTELS.COM

BORGO DI VAGLI
MERCATALE DI CORTONA
TEL.: 0575 619650
WWW.TUSCANY-GOLDCROWN.COM

HOTEL TORRE DI BELLOSGUARDO
VIA ROTI MICHELOZZI, 2 ⁕ FLORENCE
TEL.: 055 2298145
WWW.TORREBELLOSGUARDO.COM

ACQUAMATTA
PIAZZA DELLA VITTORIA, 13
CAPOLONA, OUTSIDE AREZZO
TEL.: 0575 420999

DA DELFINA
VIA DELLA CHIESA, 1 ✣ ARTIMINO
TEL.: 055 8718074

DA NERBONE
PORK'S
Both are inside the San Lorenzo market
in Florence. Lunch only.

FONTELUNGA
C.S. MONTALLA, 747
MONTANARE DI CORTONA
TEL.: 0575 62464
WWW.FONTELUNGA.IT
Restaurant plus residences for rent. Cooking school.

I TRE BICCHIERI
PIAZZETTA SOPRA I PONTI, 3,4,5 ✣ AREZZO
TEL.: 0575 26557
Also a wine bar serving forty wines from the Arezzo
province, and four hundred others.

MONDO X: IL RISTORANTE DELLA FRATERIA
CONVENTO DI SAN FRANCESCO ✣ CETONA
TEL.: 0578 238015
WWW.LAFRATERIA.IT
Valter is in the kitchen; you're in good hands. They
also have rooms, if you would like peace and seclusion.

OSTERIA DEL TEATRO
VIA MAFFEI, 2 ✣ CORTONA
TEL.: 0575 630556

TRATTORIA MIMMI
MERCATALE DI CORTONA
TEL.: 0575 619092

TRATTORIA TOSCANA
VIA DARDANO, 12 ✣ CORTONA
TEL.: 0575 604192

RELAIS IL FALCONIERE
LOCALITÀ SAN MARTINO, 370 ✣ CORTONA
TEL.: 0575 612616
WWW.ILFALCONIERE.COM
A Relais & Chateaux hotel and restaurant with
cooking school and wine tasting week.

GARDENS

These are the gardens described in the text. Verify opening
times before visiting.

VILLA CETINALE
SOVICILLE, NEAR SIENA
TEL.: 0577 311147
WWW.CETINALE-MANOR.IT
The garden is open Monday through Friday, 9:30 to 12
noon. Telephone for a reservation.

VILLA LA GAMBERAIA
VIA DEL ROSSELLINO, 72
SETTIGNANO, NEAR FLORENCE
TEL.: 055 697205
Open daily by appointment. There are three apartments for
rent. For information, call 055 697090.

VILLA LA FOCE
STRADA DELLA VITTORIA, 61
53042 CHIANCIANO TERME
TEL.: 0578 69101
Guided visits at varying times. Call for information.

VILLA DELLA PETRAIA
VIA DI PETRAIA, 40
CASTELLO, NEAR FLORENCE
TEL.: 055 452691
Open daily but call for hours.

VILLA DEL CASTELLO
VIA DI CASTELLO, 44
CASTELLO, NEAR VILLA PETRAIA
TEL.: 055 454791
Open daily but call for hours.

VILLA CORSINI
VIA DI CASTELLO, BETWEEN VILLA PETRAIA AND VILLA
DEL CASTELLO
CASTELLO
TEL.: 055 23575
Call for information.

LIBRE

BOOKS

Images and Shadows, by Iris Origo

Italian Villas and Their Gardens, by Edith Wharton

The Gardens of Pompeii, Herculaneum, and the Villas Destroyed by Vesuvius, by Wilhelmina Jashemski

Gardens of Pompeii, by Annamaria Ciarallo

Italian Dreams, by Steven Rothfeld

La Foce: A Garden and Landscape in Tuscany, by Benedetta Origo, et al.

Letters of the Younger Pliny, edited by Betty Radice

Marcus Porcius Cato on Agriculture: Marcus Terentius Varro on Agriculture, edited by William Davis Hooper, et al.

The Garden Lover's Guide to Italy, by Penelope Hobhouse

The Medici Villas, by Isabella Lapi Ballerini

Prospero's Cell, by Lawrence Durrell

Shrines, by Steven Rothfeld

War in the Val d'Orcia, by Iris Origo